NICK SWETTENHAM

The Big 500 - 1980s Music Trivia and Fun Facts

Embrace the Nostalgia of the 80s By Testing Your Knowledge and History of Classic Pop, Rock, New Wave, Hip Hop and More!

First published by Nick Swettenham 2022

Copyright © 2022 by Nick Swettenham

All rights reserved. No part of this publication may be reproduced, stored or transmitted in any form or by any means, electronic, mechanical, photocopying, recording, scanning, or otherwise without written permission from the publisher. It is illegal to copy this book, post it to a website, or distribute it by any other means without permission.

Nick Swettenham asserts the moral right to be identified as the author of this work.

Nick Swettenham has no responsibility for the persistence or accuracy of URLs for external or third-party Internet Websites referred to in this publication and does not guarantee that any content on such Websites is, or will remain, accurate or appropriate.

Designations used by companies to distinguish their products are often claimed as trademarks. All brand names and product names used in this book and on its cover are trade names, service marks, trademarks and registered trademarks of their respective owners. The publishers and the book are not associated with any product or vendor mentioned in this book. None of the companies referenced within the book have endorsed the book.

First edition

This book was professionally typeset on Reedsy. Find out more at reedsy.com

Contents

Introduction	1
Chapter 1 - General Pop Music	4
Round 1	6
Round 1 Answers	10
Round 2	12
Round 2 Answers	16
Round 3	18
Round 3 Answers	22
Round 4	24
Round 4 Answers	27
Round 5 – Lyric Test	29
Round 5 Answers	32
Bonus Guitar lesson 1	33
Bonus Guitar Lesson 2	35
Chapter 2 - New Wave, Synth Pop and New Romantic	37
Round 1	39
Round 1 Answers	42
Round 2	43
Round 2 Answers	46
Round 3	48
Round 3 Answers	52
Round 4 – Lyric Test	53
Round 4 Answers	56
Bonus Guitar Lesson 3	57
Chapter 3 - Say My Name	59

Say My Name Answers	63
Chapter 4 - Rock	64
Round 1	66
Round 1 Answers	69
Round 2	71
Round 2 Answers	74
Round 3	76
Round 3 Answers	80
Round 4 – Lyric Test	81
Round 4 Answers	85
Bonus Guitar Lesson 4	86
Chapter 5 - Indie/Alternative and Post-Punk Era	88
Round 1	90
Round 1 Answers	94
Round 2	95
Round 2 Answers	99
Round 3	100
Round 3 Answers	104
Round 4 – Lyric Test	105
Round 4 Answers	109
Bonus Guitar Lesson 5	110
Chapter 6 - Film and Television	112
Round 1	113
Round 1 Answers	116
Round 2	117
Round 2 Answers	120
Round 3	122
Round 3 Answers	125
Chapter 7 - Metal, Glam and Thrash	127
Round 1	128
Round 1 Answers	131

Round 2	133
Round 2 Answers	137
Round 3 – Lyric Test	138
Round 3 Answers	141
Bonus Guitar Lesson 6	142
Chapter 8 - Music Video	144
Music Video Answers	148
Chapter 9 - Reggae/Ska	150
Round 1	151
Round 1 Answers	155
Round 2	156
Round 2 Answers	159
Round 3 – Lyric Test	161
Round 3 Answers	164
Bonus Guitar Lesson 7	165
Chapter 10 - Soul/R&B	167
Round 1	168
Round 1 Answers	171
Round 2	173
Round 2 Answers	177
Round 3 – Lyric Test	178
Round 3 Answers	181
Bonus Guitar Lesson 8	182
Chapter 11 - Album Cover Description	184
Album Covers Answers	188
Bonus Guitar Lesson 9	189
Chapter 12 – Hip-Hop And Early Gangsta Rap	191
Round 1	193
Round 1 Answers	197
Round 2	199
Round 2 Answers	202

Round 3 – Lyric Test	204
Round 3 Answers	207
Chapter 13 - Big events, Awards and Chart Toppers	208
Big events, Awards and Chart Toppers Answers	211
10 Final Fun Facts About the 1980s	213
Bonus Guitar Lesson 10	216
Chapter 14 - What Comes Next?	218
Where To Find Me	220

Introduction

The 1980s was one of the most unique, creative and fun decades in pop culture history. It was the decade that brought with it the advent of MTV, CDs, Camcorders and Apple computers, to name just a few.

The 80s were a much more prosperous time than the 1970s. In the USA, the 70s was a period of social revolution, economic recession and mass skepticism in politicians following the Watergate scandal in the early part of the decade. The Vietnam war was an incredibly divisive issue, and not winning the war left America with a feeling of uncertainty and a lack of confidence as a nation. Oil prices and inflation were skyrocketing both in the United States and across the Pond in the United Kingdom, where worker strikes were becoming commonplace. Overall, it was a tumultuous period to live in.

This uncertainty had a knock-on effect on pop culture, as the movies and music reflected these themes. Rock 'n' Roll music was often grittier and more self-reflective than the music of the 60s. Punk music was heavy, fast and anti-establishment. Whilst Disco, Soul and Funk had a more optimistic vibe and were hugely successful, there was definitely a change in the air towards the end of the 70s. So how did the stark contrast in music between the 1970s and 1980s come around?

THE BIG 500 - 1980S MUSIC TRIVIA AND FUN FACTS

The 80s became a period of huge economic growth in the USA but more importantly, cultural change. On December 8th 1980, John Lennon was tragically shot dead. This, for many, symbolically marked an end of the 60s and 70s era of activism and idealism that he represented. Just a few weeks prior to Lennon's passing, Ronald Reagan was elected president of the United States. These were two incredibly important moments in history that would help to usher in this new decade, together with a major pop culture moment from the former decade. In the summer of 1977, Star Wars was released in theaters and became the highest-grossing film of all time. This opened the door for a whole new world of filmmaking in the 1980s, which led to a huge sense of optimism and adventure.

As the politics and culture changed, so did the music. With a new sense of optimism, economic growth and technological advances in music, the 1980s began to blossom. The 1980s opened up a kaleidoscope of musical genres and subgenres. Although synthesizers had been around since as early as the late 1950s, the 1980s was truly the decade of the synth! It was prominent in multiple genres of music, which is one of the reasons why 80s music is so distinctive.

Mainstream Pop music reflected the times and was seen by many as a decade of shallowness and materialism. Musicians were becoming incredibly rich and displaying this wealth became fashionable - this made Pop music vibrant, fun and gave Western society a feeling of escapism and that anything was possible. This was reflected in the now-famous 80s fashion... actually, let's not go there! Other genres of music such as Indie/Alternative, Punk and Hip Hop spoke up for the underclasses and provided the social commentary that most mainstream music was lacking at the time. All these elements made for a truly diverse decade of incredible musical accomplishments.

INTRODUCTION

On a personal note and as a songwriter myself, I have been influenced by so much 80s music. Being born in 1983, a lot of my first memories of music were from bands like Tears for Fears, R.E.M, Simple Minds, The Cure, The Smiths and so many more. For me, listening to music from this period induces a sense of nostalgia that cannot be replicated.

I want this book to reflect the spirit of the 80s, and pay tribute to not only mainstream Pop and Rock music, but also other important genres that have had chart success and deserve recognition. It's impossible to cover everything as the 80s opened up so many musical doors, but I'll try my best to do it justice. Unfortunately, I won't be covering genres like Classical Music, Underground Dance and Jazz as they rarely had songs that made it into the charts. However, I do hope you, the reader, will not only be able to test your knowledge on this amazing decade of music but also learn some new fun facts that you might not have known before.

We will look at each main genre of music, starting with general Pop. *Bear in mind, some questions will cover more than one genre in this chapter.* We will then move on to more specific genres that will become more challenging depending on your taste in music. The more popular the genre during the decade, the more rounds we'll have.

By the end of this book, you'll feel like an 80s music expert and most likely bore your friends and family with your new wealth of knowledge (I say this from first-hand experience)! I hope you enjoy the ride.

Let's get started!

Chapter 1 - General Pop Music

"No matter who you are, no matter what you did, no matter where you've come from, you can always change, become a better version of yourself" - Madonna

What is Pop music?

It's a difficult one to define! According to The Oxford Learner's Dictionary, Pop music is:

"Popular music of the sort that has been popular since the 1950s, usually with a strong rhythm and simple tunes, often contrasted with rock, soul and other forms of popular music".

This definition has somewhat changed in recent decades, as Pop music these days tends to be associated with a more manufactured type of music, where performers and artists are often used as the face of Pop songs written by multiple Ghostwriters. The 1980s is seen as the start of this shift, although a huge amount of Pop artists still wrote their own songs or had a songwriting partnership.

Many Pop artists in the 80s gained popularity due to their exposure on MTV. With the emphasis, therefore, shifting towards the visual appeal, as well as musical, many musicians and groups started paying much

CHAPTER 1 - GENERAL POP MUSIC

more attention to their appearance and choreography. In the latter half of the decade, Teen Pop (Pop music specifically marketed towards pre-teens and teenagers) emerged for the first time. Many of the Pop songs of the 1980s are now classed as classics!

Any band or solo artist can produce a pop single that transcends musical genres and defines a moment in Pop culture history. Every musical genre in this book will, to some degree, be seen as Pop, as the bands and artists were hugely successful and often chart-toppers.

For this first chapter, the questions I have chosen are mostly about artists that are defined as 'Pop' when searched on Google or Spotify. There are, of course crossovers, and as we delve into the sub-genres of pop after this chapter, you will notice how the questions become more specific (dare I say, niche?) to that genre.

So without further ado, here is our first Pop Music round!

Ready?

Round 1

1. Michael Jackson's number 1 hit album 'Bad' was released in which year?

- A. 1985
- B. 1986
- C. 1987
- D. 1988

Fun Fact

Hollywood director Martin Scorsese, famous for such films as Goodfellas, Taxi Driver and Casino, directed the video for 'Bad'. The full video runs 18 minutes long and stars a young Wesley Snipes and the antagonist.

2. Madonna and Prince sang a duet together on which song on her 1989 album 'Like A Prayer'?

- A. Promise To Try
- B. Love Song
- C. Dear Jessie
- D. Spanish Eyes

ROUND 1

Fun Fact

Before making it big, Madonna worked at Dunkin' Donuts in the Big Apple whilst trying to become a professional dancer. She was apparently fired for squirting jam in a customer's face.

3. Which single gave Tina Turner her first and only number 1 Billboard 100 single selling over 1.5 million copies worldwide?

- A. What's Love Got To Do With It
- B. The Best
- C. Proud Mary
- D. Private Dancer

4. 'Dancing In The Street' was a duet by which two British artists?

Fun Fact

The song was originally written by Marvin Gaye, Ivy Jo Hunter and Mickey Stevenson and was released by Martha Reeves And The Vandellas in 1964 reaching number 2 on the US Billboard.

5. Which former Genesis member knocked the Genesis single 'Invisible Touch' off the number 1 slot on the US Billboard chart in the summer of 1986 and with which song?

6. 'I'm Still Standing' was a hit by which British artist and in what year?

- A. 1981
- B. 1983
- C. 1985
- D. 1987

7. The hit single 'Never Gonna Give You Up' by Rick Astley reached number 1 in how many countries?

- A. 12
- B. 17
- C. 25
- D. 26

Fun Fact

The song was written by Matt Aitken, Mike Stock and Peter Waterman. Legend has it that the song was inspired by a girlfriend of Pete Waterman. Astley was staying at Waterman's house and after a three hour call with the lady, Astley said the words " You're never gonna give her up". The rest is history.

8. What 80s British Pop group is named after an alcoholic beverage?

ROUND 1

9. The song 'Billie Jean' featured on which Michael Jackson album?

- A. Bad
- B. Thriller
- C. Off The Wall
- D. Dangerous

10. 'Uptown Girl' was an original hit written and sung by?

Round 1 Answers

1. 1987
2. Love Song
3. What's Love Got To Do With It
4. David Bowie and Mick Jagger
5. Peter Gabriel - Sledgehammer
6. Elton John 1983
7. 25
8. Bucks Fizz
9. Thriller
10. Billy Joel

Fun Fact

Elton John's real name is Reginald Kenneth Dwight. On February 24th 1987 he won the Grammy for 'Best Pop Performance by duo or group with vocal' for the hit song 'That's What Friends Are For' with Stevie Wonder, Gladys Knight and Dionne Warwick.

ROUND 1 ANSWERS

Fun Fact

Billy Joel was seen as a pioneer for being the first American Pop act to perform for the Soviet Union in 1987. However, this is not technically true. In 1979 Elton John performed eight concerts between 21st - 28th May. However, this takes nothing away from the historical significance as The Soviet Union had banned American pop music for so long. This was seen as a huge olive branch by embracing Americana and finally giving its citizens more freedom to express themselves.

Round 2

1. 'Eternal Flame' was a 1988 hit sung by which pop group?

2. The 1980s had so many memorable pop hits. Which song spent the longest on the US Billboard chart in the number 1 position, thus becoming the most successful single of the decade?

- A. Eye Of The Tiger - Survivor
- B. Every Breath You Take - The Police
- C. Physical - Olivia Newton-John
- D. Bette Davis Eyes - Kim Carnes

3. Which Artist had 27 hit single releases in the 1980s?

- A. Michael Jackson
- B. Diana Ross
- C. Madonna
- D. David Bowie

4. 'Born In The USA' was a huge hit by Bruce Springsteen. Which

ROUND 2

presidential candidate used the song on the campaign trail?

Fun fact

Although this candidate endorsed Bruce Springsteen and his song, the feeling was not mutual and Springsteen did not endorse this candidate.

5. 'Ebony and Ivory' was a hit single in 1982 by Paul McCartney and featured which guest artist?

- A. Stevie Wonder
- B. Sting
- C. Lionel Richie
- D. Barry White

6. Name these two 'Phil's' Who collaborated on the 1984/1985 hit 'Easy Lover'?

- A. Phil Collins
- B. Phil Lesh
- C. Phil Bailey
- D. Phil Keaggy

7. Chris De Burgh's 'Lady in Red' was from which album?

- A. Flying Colors
- B. The Getaway
- C. Best Moves
- D. Into The Light

Fun Fact

Lady In Red was actually written about his wife Diana after having an argument. He was originally going to call the song 'The Way You Look Tonight' but that title was already a classic by Rat pack legend Frank Sinatra. He then found his title after seeing Diana from a distance in a crowded nightclub wearing a red dress.

8. Which album was the highest selling by a female artist in the USA during the 1980s?

- A. Madonna - Like a Virgin
- B. Whitney Houston - Whitney Houston
- C. Paula Abdul - Forever Your Girl
- D. Tracy Chapman - Tracy Chapman

9. Complete the lyrics to this 1989 hit by 'Martika'

"We all fall down like ____ _____"

ROUND 2

Fun Fact

The song reached number 1 on the US Billboard charts for 2 weeks. The song's popularity led to rapper Eminem using the chorus as a sample to a song on his 2004 album 'Encore'

10. What was Kylie Minogue's debut single?

- A. I Should Be So Lucky
- B. Je Ne Sais Pas Pourquoi
- C. The Loco-Motion
- D. Got To Be Certain

Fun Fact

Before she was a Pop megastar, Kylie played Charlene Mictchell on the Australian soap opera 'Neighbours' in 1986. She later returned alongside Jason Donovan for the soap's final episode in 2022.

Round 2 Answers

1. The Bangles
2. Physical - Olivia Newton-John
3. Diana Ross
4. Ronald Reagan
5. Stevie Wonder
6. Phil Collins and Phil Bailey
7. Into The Light
8. Whitney Houston - Whitney Houston
9. Toy Soldiers
10. The Loco-Motion

Fun Fact

The Bangles were originally a Rock band that played their own instruments and came together through their love of The Beatles. They were called 'The Colors' and then 'The Bangs'. Although they wrote the majority of their songs, their first four Top 10 hits were not written by them. Eternal Flame was written by band member Susanna Hoffs who recorded her vocals to the song *completely naked. The song was the highest selling single ever by an all-girl band at the time.*

Fun Fact

Diana Ross was also inducted into the Rock 'N' Roll Hall Of Fame in 1988 with The Supremes, but in the 1980s she also had her own line of pantyhose called 'Diana Ross Ultra Sheers'.

Round 3

1. Name the third studio album released by Huey Lewis And The News in 1983.

   - A. Sports
   - B. Huey Lewis And The News
   - C. Fore
   - D. Picture This

2. Michael Jackson was not the only Jackson to have huge success in the 1980s. Can you name his sibling who released multiple albums, including the 1986 album 'Control'?

Fun Fact

When Marvel comics filed for bankruptcy, Michael Jackson attempted to purchase the comic book company. He wanted to take control and cast himself as Spiderman. Stan Lee, Marvel and many fans were against this due to a lack of acting experience and they didn't believe Jackson was a good fit for the part. The acquisition never happened and Marvel started to achieve major success when they cast Toby Maguire years later.

ROUND 3

3. The bands Foreigner and The Clash both have lead guitarists with the same name. Can you name them?

4. Roxette were a Pop Rock group from which country?

Fun Fact

Roxette were both established artists before they joined forces. Their first major worldwide hit 'The Look' only found success in The USA after an American exchange student by the name of Dean Cushman managed to get the song airtime on his local radio station, which then spread all around the country.

5. What was the first single released from The Bee Gees 1987 album E.S.P?

- A. The Longest Night
- B. Giving Up The Ghost
- C. You Win Again
- D. Angela

Fun Fact

This is a fun fact that you wouldn't be able to look up. In the 1970s Barry Gibb put forward my father, Geoff Swettenham, former drummer of 60s band 'Grapefruit' to become the Bee Gees drummer. Unfortunately, the other two brothers, Robin and Maurice, felt it best to keep the band strictly in the family.

6. Who was the lead singer for the band The Boomtown Rats?

7. 'It's Raining Again' and 'My Kind Of Lady' are both hit singles from which 1982 Supertramp album?

- A. Free As A Bird
- B. Famous Last Words
- C. Paris
- D. Brother Where You Bound

8. In 1980, Queen released their eighth studio album 'The Game'. They had their first US Billboard number 1 hit single from this album. It was written as a tribute to two of Freddie Mercury's heroes, Elvis Presley and Sir Cliff Richard. What was the song called?

Fun Fact

The song only took Freddie around 5 - 10 minutes to write. He was quoted in a Melody Maker interview on May 2nd 1981 stating...

"I did that on the guitar, which I can't play for nuts, and in one way, it was quite a good thing because I was restricted, knowing only a few chords. It's a good discipline because I simply had to write within a small framework. I couldn't work through too many chords and because of that restriction I wrote a good song, I think" - Freddie Mercury

ROUND 3

9. Which Pop group is best known for their 1986 hits ' Breakout', 'Surrender' and 'Twilight World'

10. British Pop band 'The Fine Young Cannibals' are best known for which hit single?

Round 3 Answers

1. Sports
2. Janet Jackson
3. Mick Jones
4. Swedish
5. You Win Again
6. Bob Geldof
7. Famous Last Words
8. Crazy Little Thing Called Love
9. Swing Out Sister
10. She Drives Me Crazy

Fun Fact

Huey Lewis And The News sued Ray Parker Jr for ripping off their song 'I Want A New Drug' with the title soundtrack song for the 1984 film 'Ghostbusters'. If you listen to them both, you can notice just how similar they are.

ROUND 3 ANSWERS

Fun Fact

Mick Jones also played guitar on the Elvis Costello song 'Big Tears' which was a B-side for 'Pump It Up'

Round 4

1. Which American singer-songwriter released the following songs in the 1980s?

   - That's Why I'm Here
   - Only A Dream In Rio
   - Never Die Young

2. Complete the names of this four-piece Folk Rock super group

Crosby, _____, Nash & _____

3. The names 'Jane' and 'Maggie' both feature in song titles by which UK solo artist? Can you also name the full song titles and which of the two hits was released in the 1980s?

4. In 1980 Barbra Streisand and Barry Gibb teamed up to record their first duet together and in 1981 won the Grammy award for best Pop performance by a duo or group with vocals. What was the name of his hit?

ROUND 4

5. In 1986 Bananarama released a hit single that is named after a planet in our solar system. Name the planet and you name the song.

Fun Fact

This single was a huge success reaching number 1 in the US and Australia as well as number 8 in the UK. However, like a lot of modern Pop songs, it was a cover of the 1969 song by Shocking Blue.

6. Haysi Fantayzee were a short-lived Pop band but they did have a couple of hit singles in the early part of the decade. One of them is a song with an actor's name in the title. Can you complete the title by naming this famous actor?

"_____ _____ Is Big Leggy"

7. Before his momentous solo career, George Michael found fame and fortune in the Pop duo Wham. Who was his partner in crime?

8. Which of the following bands released the hit soft Rock Pop single 'I'm All Out Of Love' in 1980?

- A. Toto
- B. Air Supply
- C. Genesis
- D. Foreigner

9. Which artist wrote the following 80s hits?

- Back In The High Life
- Higher Love
- Valerie

10. Name the number 1 US single that held that position for 3 weeks in 1985 by Pop Rock band 'REO Speedwagon' from the 1984 album 'Wheels Are Turning'?

Fun Fact

REO performed the song at Band Aid in 1985 and were introduced by Chevy Chase.

Round 4 Answers

1. James Taylor
2. Stills and Young
3. Rod Stewart, Baby Jane 1983 and Maggie May 1971
4. Guilty
5. Venus
6. John Wayne
7. Andrew Ridgeley
8. Air Supply
9. Steve Winwood
10. Can't Fight This Feeling Anymore

Fun Fact

James Taylor began by playing the Cello and wrote this song at the age of 14. He was signed to The Beatles record label 'Apple' at one point and has 40 multi-platinum, platinum and gold records along with 5 Grammy awards.

Fun Fact

Rod Stewart has always had a penchant for women and particularly models. He's dated two Bond girls, Kelly Emberg and Britt Ekland. He's been married three times. Alana Stewart from 1979 - 1984, Rachel Hunter 1990 – 2006 and Penny Lancaster since 2007. He also apparently stated once that he would rather cut off his penis than cheat on Rachel Hunter. Now that's love!

Fun Fact

During the mid 1980's China was still very cut off from the west due to the actions of the far-left Communist dictator Mao Zedong. Music, in particular, was banned but Wham became the first Pop act to perform in China in front of 15,000 people at the People's Gymnasium in Beijing in April 1985.

Fun Fact

Air Supply met whilst performing in the Australian 'Jesus Chris Superstar'. They all shared a love for The Beatles and that's what brought them together and kept them together since 1975.

Round 5 – Lyric Test

Guess the song and artist by reading their words of wisdom.

Song 1

"You put the boom-boom into my heart (ooh-ooh)
 You send my soul sky-high
 When your lovin' starts"

Song 2

"I was beat
 Incomplete
 I'd been had, I was sad and blue
 But you made me feel
 Yeah, you made me feel
 Shiny and new"

Song 3

"I've done alright up to now
  It's the light of day that shows me how
  And when the night falls, loneliness calls"

Song 4

"Now I don't want u back for the weekend
  Not back for a day, no no no
  I said baby I just want you back and I want you to stay
  Woah yeah!"

Song 5

"Poor old Johnnie Ray
  Sounded sad upon the radio
  Moved a million hearts in mono
  Our mothers cried
  Sang along, who'd blame them?"

Song 6

"Maybe you're just like my mother
  She's never satisfied (she's never satisfied)
  Why do we scream at each other?
  This is what it sounds like"

ROUND 5 – LYRIC TEST

Song 7

"(Turn around)
  Every now and then I get a little bit lonely
  And you're never coming 'round"

Song 8

"All I know is that to me
  You look like you're havin' fun
  Open up your lovin' arms
  Watch out, here I come"

Song 9

"You've been around all night and that's a little long
  You think you've got the right but I think you've got it wrong
  Why can't you say goodnight?
  So you can take me home"

Song 10

"In my life, there's been heartache and pain
  I don't know if I can face it again
  Can't stop now, I've traveled so far
  To change this lonely life"

Round 5 Answers

1. Wake Me Up Before You Go-Go - Wham
2. Like A Virgin - Madonna
3. I Wanna Dance With Somebody - Whitney Houston
4. Walking On Sunshine - Katrina And The Waves
5. Come On Eileen - Dexys Midnight Runners
6. When Doves Cry - Prince
7. Total Eclipse Of The Heart - Bonnie Tyler
8. You Spin Me Round (Like A Record) - Dead Or Alive
9. Mickey - Toni Basil
10. I Want To Know What Love Is - Foreigner

Bonus Guitar lesson 1

Scan the novelty sized QR code on the next page for your first
Bonus Guitar lesson:
Introduction Video Part One

THE BIG 500 - 1980S MUSIC TRIVIA AND FUN FACTS

Bonus Guitar Lesson 2

Scan the novelty sized QR code on the next page for your second
Bonus Guitar lesson:
Introduction Video Part Two

THE BIG 500 - 1980S MUSIC TRIVIA AND FUN FACTS

Chapter 2 - New Wave, Synth Pop and New Romantic

"I have always been far more interested in sound than technique, and how sounds work together, how they can be layered. I think electronic music, in its infancy anyway, allowed us to create music in a way that hadn't really been possible before. It created a new kind of musician" - Gary Numan

New Wave, Synth Pop and New Romantic music are all heavily influenced by the Punk movement of the 1970s. As the 80s rolled around, however, songs in these genres became far more commercial. As the decade progressed, the sounds gradually changed until they became almost unrecognizable as having originated from the Punk era of the 70s.

New Wave became an umbrella term that covered multiple music genres, and Synth Pop is probably its main subgenre. As the name suggests, the artists and bands creating Synth Pop music used heavy synthesizers to produce this unique sound. This genre is incredibly distinctive and has provided some of the biggest and most nostalgic hits of the 1980s that we still love today.

New Romantic was originally an underground movement in the UK during the late 70s, but it built itself into the mainstream charts during the 1980s. Fashion-wise, it was influenced by 1970s Glam Rock, fashion labels like Kahn and Bell and PX, and also the Romantic Era of the late 18th and early 19th century. There is no distinct sound to the New Romantic movement - listening to these songs, you would usually associate them with New Wave and Synth Pop. It's more the visual style that defines them, with New Romantic music being that much more flamboyant in both fashion and make up.

Many of the artists you'll be quizzed on in this chapter cross over multiple subgenres, as they are very intertwined. Much like chapter 1, the questions in this chapter still cover incredibly mainstream music, so hopefully, you'll be scoring high marks!

Ready?

Round 1

1. Which British pop synth duo is formed of Chris Lowe and Neil Tennant?

2. Frankie went to _____ and told us to _____ in 1983?

3. Which band wrote the hit song 'Don't You Want Me'?

- A. Depeche Mode
- B. Human League
- C. Erasure
- D. Duran Duran

Fun Fact

The band in question's name was taken from the Sci-Fi board game' Star Force' and one of the empires was the answer to the previous question. The Band was previously called The Future.

4. Which classic 1981 Kraftwerk song's melody was used by Coldplay for the 2005 song 'Talk'?

Fun fact

The Kraftwerk song in the previous question was released twice in the same year. It only peaked at number 36 in the UK before its second release in November 1981. This time it was a double A-side single along with the song 'The Model'

5. Which 'New Order' song would make you think of going back to work after the weekend?

6. Name the 80s Synth- Pop band who wrote these 3 popular 1980s songs

- A Little Respect
- Oh L'Amour
- Sometimes

7. What year was 'The Eurythmics' song 'Sweet Dreams (Are Made Of This)' released?

- A. 1981
- B. 1983
- C. 1985
- D. 1987

ROUND 1

Fun Fact

'Sweet Dreams (Are Made Of This)' was the first ever Eurythmics single to be released in the United States. It started at a mere number 90 but by August of that year, it reached number 2 for four weeks before it made it to the number 1 slot. The Song also reached number 2 in the UK and is known as their breakthrough single.

8. Which British Synth Pop band released the hit single 'Tainted Love' in 1981?

Fun Fact

This version of Tainted Love is actually a cover. The original recording was as early as 1964 by Gloria Jones and written and produced by Ed Cobb. It was released in 1965 but failed to reach the charts in either the US or UK. She re-released the song in 1976 due to the song's sound fitted perfectly with the Northern Soul movement of the 70s. Unfortunately, the song flopped again and only became an international hit after its 1981 Synth Pop release.

9. Danny Elfman became known for his soundtracks to films like Batman, Good Will Hunting and The Nightmare Before Christmas but before that, he formed a New Wave band that had a hit single 'Weird Science' In 1985. Can you name this band?

10. Which New Wave Band were named after a type of bird and known for their ridiculous hairstyles?

Round 1 Answers

1. The Pet Shop Boys
2. Frankie went to Hollywood and told us to Relax
3. Human League
4. Computer Love
5. Blue Monday
6. Erasure
7. 1983
8. Soft Cell
9. Oingo Boingo
10. A Flock Of Seagulls

Fun Fact

The music video for the Pet Shop Boys 1988 hit song 'Heart' starred none other than Sir Ian McKellen.

Round 2

1. Which Pioneering New Wave band released the song 'Atomic' in 1980?

Fun Fact

During the height of the Britpop era, the Indie band Sleeper recorded their own version of 'Atomic' for the 1996 film 'Trainspotting' starring Ewan McGregor.

2. Duran Duran's Nick Rhodes famously co-produced the band Kajagoogoo's first single and in January 1983, it went to number 1 in the UK. What was the name of this chart topper?

- A. Hang On Now
- B. Too Shy
- C. Ooh To Be Aah
- D. Big Apple

Fun Fact

This hit song was also produced by Duran Duran's producer Colin Thurston and reached number 1 before any of Duran Duran's singles.

3. Which US politician inspired the New Wave/ Goth album 'Vision Thing' by Sisters of Mercy with the quote 'The Vision Thing' ahead of the 1988 US presidential election?

4. In 1984 The Cars released their fifth studio album 'Heartbreak City'. The album boasted their highest-selling single to date in most countries. Can you name it? The band's name is a hint to the title of this song.

5. Name the final album released by The Cure in the 1980s.

- A. Disintegration
- B. The Head On The Door
- C. Wish
- D. Kiss Me, Kiss Me, Kiss Me

6. What was the name of Gary Numan's second studio album in 1980?

Fun Fact

Gary Numan was originally in the Punk Rock band Tubeway Army. However, after signing a record deal to record a Punk album, he had his first go at the synthesizer and the sound changed dramatically. Tubeway Army would become the first band to have a synth-based number 1 single with 'Are Friends

ROUND 2

Electric'

7. The New Wave band Joy Division only released two studio albums before lead singer Ian Curtis tragically took his own life on the eve of their first North American tour. Their first studio album was released in 1979 titled 'Unknown Pleasures'. Can you name their second?

8. Can you name the two founding members of Tears For Fears?

9. Name the New Wave band formed in Athens, Georgia, USA that is named after an American long-range, jet-powered bomber.

10. Which English New Wave band released the world's first cassette single 'C30 C60 C90 Go' in 1980?

Round 2 Answers

1. Blonde
2. Too Shy
3. George H. W Bush
4. Drive
5. Disintegration
6. Telekon
7. Closer (1980)
8. Roland Orzabal and Curt Smith
9. The B-52's
10. Bow Wow Wow

Fun Fact

Duran Duran became so popular in the 80s that in 1985 Milton Bradley released a Duran Duran board game called 'Into The Arena'

Fun Fact

The B-52's are from Athens, Georgia, USA. R.E.M, Drive-By Truckers and The Black Crowes are all formed in the same city. Katie Pierson would later

ROUND 2 ANSWERS

work with REM on the 1991 hit single 'Shining Happy People'.

Round 3

1. In 1987 Belinda Carlisle had a number 1 US Billboard hit 'Heaven Is A Place On Earth' but which all-girl New Wave band was she in before her solo career?

Fun Fact

Belinda Carlisle was actually a drummer in the Punk band The Germs before she became a singer. She would then go on to form the group The Misfits. They soon changed their name to become the band in the previous question. They also became the first all-female band in history to achieve a US Billboard number 1 album in 1981.

2. In 1983 The German New Wave band Nena released the song '99 LuftBallons'. Later that year, they released it in English. What does the original title translate to?

3. Complete the full name of the New Wave band OMD

Orchestral _____ In The _____

ROUND 3

4. The following 3 songs are by which New Wave band?

- Love My Way
- Pretty In Pink
- The Ghost In You

5. Which Eurythmics album did the hit single 'There Must Be An Angel' feature on?

- A. Be Yourself Tonight
- B. Touch
- C. In The Garden
- D. Revenge

Fun Fact

The Eurythmics was actually formed in an Australian town called Wagga Wagga. Annie Lennox and Dave Stewart were previously in a band called The Tourists. They had some success in Australia with a cover of the Dusty Springfield song 'I Only Wanna Be With You' reaching number 6 in the charts. They were stuck in this town on their way to Sidney when they started experimenting more with the synthesizer and the rest is history!

6. Which song is heavily associated with The Human League but was actually originally released by the band's singer/songwriter Philip Oakey along with Italian composer Georgio Moroder?

7. Which song gave Cindy Lauper her first number 1 single on the US Billboard chart?

- A. Time After Time
- B. Girls Just Wanna Have Fun
- C. True Colors
- D. I Drove All Night

8. Which New Wave band had a distinctive line up featuring two sets of brothers? The Mothersbaughs brother and the Casales brothers. They also had a number 14 hit single on the US Billboard 'Whip it'.

9. Which Depeche Mode single was known as their international breakthrough song and became an anthem for the gay community?

- A. Boys Say Go
- B. Nothing To Fear
- C. A Question Of Lust
- D. People Are People

Fun Fact

Vince Clark was the band's main songwriter boasting 9 of the songs on their debut album, including the single 'Just Can't Get Enough'. He quit the band the same year and Martin Gore took over as the main writer.

ROUND 3

10. Complete the 1985 song by the band Tears For Fears

'Everybody wants to _____ _____ _____'

Fun Fact

Curt Smith created the band's name after the statement in Janov's 1980 book 'Prisoners Of Pain' which read, "tears as a replacement for fears"

Round 3 Answers

1. The Go-Go's
2. 99 Red Balloons
3. Orchestral Manoeuvres In The Dark (OMD)
4. The Psychedelic Furs
5. Be Yourself Tonight
6. Together In Electric Dreams
7. Time After Time
8. Devo
9. People Are People
10. Rule The World

Fun Fact

The OMD song 'If You Leave' was written for the 1986 John Hughes film 'Pretty In Pink' and featured in the final scene.

Round 4 – Lyric Test

Guess the song and artist by reading their words of wisdom.

Song 1

"Sometimes I feel I've got to run away
  I've got to get away
  From the pain, you drive into the heart of me
  The love we share seems to go nowhere"

Song 2

"We're talking away
  I don't know what
  I'm to say I'll say it anyway
  Today's another day to find you
  Shying away
  I'll be coming for your love, okay?"

Song 3

"Desert loving in your eyes all the way
　If I listen to your lies, would you say
　I'm a man (a man) without conviction
　I'm a man (a man) who doesn't know"

Song 4

"I bought a ticket to the world
　But now I've come back again
　Why do I find it hard to write the next line?
　Oh, I want the truth to be said"

Song 5

"It's time we should talk about it
　There's no secret kept in here
　Forgive me for asking
　Now wipe away your tears"

Song 6

" I used to think that the day would never come
　I'd see delight in the shade of the morning sun
　My morning sun is the drug that brings me near
　To the childhood I lost, replaced by fear"

ROUND 4 – LYRIC TEST

Song 7

"Funny how I find myself in love with you
   If I could buy my reasoning, I'd pay to lose
   One half won't do"

Song 8

"All I ever wanted
   All I ever needed
   Is here in my arms
   Words are very unnecessary
   They can only do harm"

Song 9

"I feel safest of all
   I can lock all my doors"

Song 10

"Came in from the city, walked into the door
   I turned around when I heard the sound of footsteps on the floor"

Round 4 Answers

1. Tainted Love - Soft Cell
2. Take On Me - A-Ha
3. Karma Chameleon - Culture Club
4. True - Spandau Ballet
5. Wishful Thinking - China Crisis
6. True Faith - New Order
7. It's My Life - Talk Talk
8. Enjoy The Silence - Depeche Mode
9. Cars - Gary Numan
10. Don't Go - Yazoo

Bonus Guitar Lesson 3

**Scan the novelty sized QR code on the next page for your third
Bonus Guitar lesson:
Personal Jesus by Depeche Mode**

THE BIG 500 - 1980S MUSIC TRIVIA AND FUN FACTS

Chapter 3 - Say My Name

"It was the case in the 70s and 80s that people believed music could change the world" - Sinead O'Connor

Throughout the decades, there have been countless classic songs with people's names in the title. From 'Black Betty' to 'Hey Jude' there will always be songs about a certain someone, and the 1980s is no different!

For this bonus round, all you have to do is guess the name of these 10 songs. Each song has someone's first name in the title and you get three clues on each question.

Ready?

Song 1

- An abused daughter kills her father
- She had a gun
- The band thinks it's 'Crazy' but understands 'What It Takes'

Song 2

- She claimed I was the father of her child
- She stalked me and sent me letters
- She said that 'I am the one'

Song 3

- I am also a famous Horror film
- The band is named after a continent
- I am sad power ballad written about suicide

Song 4

- Are we long-lost pals?
- My wife Peggy is now 'Betty'
- Chevy Chase is in the music video

CHAPTER 3 - SAY MY NAME

Song 5

- My name is an invention, but it's very well known
- My creator put me where he requires no jacket
- His old band is the first chapter in the Bible

Song 6

- I'm inspired by a childhood romance
- My band likes to exercise at midnight
- Johnnie Ray is very sad

Song 7

- I am a mysterious woman, cool like Jazz on a summer's day
- I was at the top of my professional game and let it all slip away
- My name has been used in many songs and I sometimes have ginger hair

Song 8

- I am a border guard in East Germany
- I have a woman's name but I'm actually a male
- The Berlin Wall keeps me apart from my Rocketman

Song 9

- I am an actress from a family of actors, one of whom loves to 'Scream'
- I dated the band's keyboard player and later went out with Peter Gabriel
- The man who wrote the song about me loves Africa

Song 10

- I was named because girls' names ending with 'A' always make great song titles
- The band are named after an east coast American City
- I was their first and only number 1 hit in 1986

Say My Name Answers

1. Janie's Got A Gun - Aerosmith 1989
2. Billie Jean - Michael Jackson 1982
3. Carrie - Europe 1986
4. You Can Call Me Al - Paul Simon 1986
5. Sussudio - Phil Collins 1985
6. Come On Eileen - Dexy's Midnight Runners 1983
7. Valerie - Steve Winwood 1982
8. Nikita - Elton John 1985
9. Rosanna - Toto 1982
10. Amanda - Boston 1986

Chapter 4 - Rock

"If you want to be a rock star or just be famous, then run down the street naked, you'll make the news or something. But if you want music to be your livelihood, then play, play, play and play! And eventually you'll get to where you want to be" - Eddie Van Halen

Rock 'N' Roll music originated in the late 1940s and early 1950s. During the 50s, it was pioneered by music legends like Chuck Berry, Little Richard, Elvis Presley and Bo Diddley. However, it was in the 1960s, when bands like The Beatles came to America, that Rock 'N' Roll became a household name globally. During the late 1960s and early 1970s Rock 'N' Roll developed into a slightly harder sound known as Rock music, or, as we call it today, "Classic Rock". This sound relied far more on electric guitars with more crunch and overdrive, long guitar solos and deeper lyrical content.

Moving into the 1980s, it was almost impossible for Rock music not to become influenced by the synthesizer technology of the time which resulted in the creation of a very unique sound. 80s Rock is often seen as cheesier than that of the previous and future decades, but the songs were also epic and powerful. In fact, the 'Power Ballad' is almost exclusively associated with the 1980s. As the decade ended, pop culture and music changed considerably. Once bands like Nirvana came along, 80s Rock

CHAPTER 4 - ROCK

became extinct almost overnight. The music industry reverted to a more gritty style of music which was less influenced by over-the-top fashion trends and synthesized music.

Some of the greatest Rock songs of all time are from the 1980s, so let's find out just how much you know!

Ready?

Round 1

1. The lead guitarist of Hard Rock band Guns and Roses is called?

2. Which Dire Straits song started with the faint background vocal line ' I want my MTV'?

Fun fact

Sting was the artist who sang that iconic line at the start of this song.

3. Which one of these 4 songs was not from an album by Fleetwood Mac in the 1980s?

- A. Gypsy
- B. Seven wonders
- C. Sisters of the moon
- D. Everywhere

ROUND 1

4. 'The Joshua Tree' was a huge groundbreaking album. Can you guess the following?

- The name of the band?
- The year of it was released?
- The nationality of the band members?

5. Which Rock guitarist featured on Michael Jackson's 'Beat It' in 1983?

6. Name the lead singer of the Rock/ Grunge band Nirvana?

Fun Fact

I know what you're thinking - Nirvana is a 90s band! Yes, even though Nirvana are heavily associated with Grunge and the early 1990s, they actually formed in Aberdeen, Washington 1987 and their first album 'Bleach' was released in 1989.

7. Which two members of Red Hot Chili Peppers both joined the band in 1988, which helped lead them to become one of the biggest bands of all time?

Fun Fact

Although one of these two members has left the band multiple times due to drug addiction issues, the four main members have reunited and toured together in 2022. I was fortunate enough to witness this firsthand.

8. Which 1980 AC/DC song has the most plays on Spotify as of 2022?

- A. Highway To Hell
- B. You Shook Me All Night Long
- C. Thunderstruck
- D. Back In Black

9. Which 1981 song by the band Rush is named after a famous Mark Twain novel?

Fun Fact

Rush currently boasts 3 multi-platinum, 14 platinum and 24 gold albums. They were inducted into the Canadian Hall of Fame in 1994 and the Rock 'N' Roll Hall of Fame in 2013.

10. Name the Rock band named after a country that released the following albums in the 1980s.

- A. Alibi
- B. View From The Ground
- C. Your Move
- D. Perspective

Round 1 Answers

1. Slash
2. Money For Nothing
3. Sisters Of The Moon
4. U2, 1987, Irish
5. Eddie Van Halen
6. Kurt Cobain
7. John Frusciante and Chad Smith
8. Black In Black
9. Tom Sawyer
10. America

Fun Fact

Slash, is not actually fully American. He was born in Hampstead, England in 1965. His father, Tony, is British and his mother, Ola, is African – American. She was a clothes designer and created outfits for the likes of The Pointer Sisters, David Bowie, Linda Ronstadt and many more. His father was also an artist, so maybe that's where his creative genes came from.

Fun Fact

In 1983 Van Halen earned a place in the Guinness Book Of Records by playing at the US Festival for an hour and a half, earning 1.5 million dollars. This was the highest a band had ever been paid for a single appearance.

Round 2

1. Which Guns and Roses hit was famously written in under 5 minutes?

- A. Welcome to the Jungle
- B. Mr. Brownstone
- C. Paradise City
- D. Sweet Child O' Mine

Fun Fact

Axl Rose and Izzy Stradlin were originally in the band Hollywood Rose. Stradlin became flatmates with Tracii Guns in 1984, who was part of the band LA Guns. The two bands came together and combined the names into the legendary band we know today.

2. Which album was the hit single 'Don't Stop Believing' by the band Journey on?

- A. Escape
- B. Departure
- C. Captured
- D. Frontiers

3. Rick Allen was the famous 'One armed drummer' from which British band?

- A. Queen
- B. Def Leppard
- C. U2
- D. Genesis

4. The hit single 'Africa' was by which American Rock band?

5. Which of these Bon Jovi songs was featured on the album 'Slippery When Wet'?

- A. To The Fire
- B. Runaway
- C. Livin' On a Prayer
- D. I'll Be there For You

Fun Fact

Bon Jovi named their second studio album '7800 degrees Fahrenheit' because it is apparently the temperature that rocks melt.

6. The 1980 AC/DC Album 'Back in Black' was the first album sung by their new lead vocalist after he replaced Bon Scott. What was his name?

ROUND 2

(Not so) Fun Fact

Tragically AD/DC's first lead vocalist Bon Scott died earlier that year from alcohol abuse at just the age of 33. He was, without a doubt, a Rock 'N' Roll legend.

7. Fill in the blank. 1987 was the year that Aerosmith released their ninth studio album titled 'Permanent _____'

8. Which English Rock band released the song 'Here I Go Again' in 1982?

9. Which American Rock band had the hit 1980s albums ' Eliminator' and 'Afterburner'?

10. Name the last album released in the 1980s by the Rock band 'Queen' that featured the songs 'Breakthru' and ' I Want It All'

Fun Fact

Although not a believer in astrology, Freddie Mercury used the astrological signs of all four band members to design the famous 'Queen Crest' used on their Greatest Hits II album in 1991.

Round 2 Answers

1. Sweet Child O' Mine
2. Escape
3. Def Leppard
4. Toto
5. Livin' On a Prayer
6. Brian Johnson
7. Vacation
8. Whitesnake
9. ZZ Top
10. The Miracle

Fun Fact

Def Leppard's 1987 'Hysteria' was their first album to feature Rick Allen's custom electric drum kit to cater to his handicap. The band was blown away at his ability to still play as well as he did with both arms.

ROUND 2 ANSWERS

Fun Fact

Toto played a huge role in Michael Jackson's 1982 album 'Thriller'. In fact, they played on almost every song on the album. Steve Porcaro even co-wrote the song 'Human Nature' with Jackson which became a top 10 single.

Fun Fact

ZZ Top turned down a 1 million dollar offer from Gillette to star in one of their adverts. They wanted the band to shave their beards. It's not surprising that they were not keen to get rid of their unique gimmick.

Round 3

1. In 1984, Bryan Adams released a hit single that was written about infidelity. Music critic Ira Robbins dubbed it a 'cheating classic'. What was its name?

- A. Heaven
- B. Run To You
- C. Summer of 69
- D. (Everything I Do) Do It For You

Fun Fact

Although the song was about cheating on your partner, the music video depicted this lust for his guitar instead.

2. In what year did Paul McCartney and Wings break up?

- A. 1980
- B. 1981
- C. 1982
- D. 1983

ROUND 3

3. Complete the name of this number 1 US billboard chart hit By the Progressive Rock band Yes in 1893

Owner of a _____ _____

Fun Fact

Yes formed in London all the way back in 1968. They have had multiple lineups throughout the decades, with a grand total of 19 full-time musicians playing for the band.

4. Mike And The Mechanics are known as a Rock Supergroup. This is largely due to their line-up of musicians, but which former Genesis member formed the band in 1985?

5. Roxy Music was formed in 1970 by Brian Ferry. The band saw great success but split up in 1983 for almost 20 years. What was the name of their final studio album released in 1982?

6. Which of the following Rolling Stones songs was released in the 1980s?

- A. It's Only Rock 'N' Roll (But I Like It)
- B. Miss You
- C. Start Me Up
- D. Shattered

Fun Fact

This song was originally meant to be for the 1978 album 'Some Girls' and was first recorded as a Reggae-Rock track. After multiple takes, they decided to hold off until they had a version they were happy with. It was then released as the classic we know and love in 1981.

7. 'I Love Rock 'N' Roll' was a huge hit in 1981, released by which Rock band?

Fun Fact

'I Love Rock 'N' Roll' was originally written and released by British band The Arrows in 1975.

8. INXS's highest-selling album was in 1987 and sold over 14 million copies worldwide. It featured the single 'New Sensation' and 'Need You Tonight'. What was the name of this classic album?

9. Complete the name of this 1984 Pretenders album. 'Learning to _____'

- A. Fly
- B. Crawl
- C. Run
- D. Walk

ROUND 3

10. How many miles would The Proclaimers walk?

Round 3 Answers

1. Run To You
2. 1981
3. Lonely Heart
4. Mike Rutherford
5. Avalon
6. Start Me Up
7. Joan Jett And The Blackhearts
8. Kick
9. Crawl
10. 500 miles

Fun Fact

'I'm Gonna Be (500 Miles)' was released in 1988 and is on the album 'Sunshine Of Leith'. It is about wanting to spend the rest of your life with a woman.

Round 4 – Lyric Test

Guess the song and artist by reading their words of wisdom.

Song 1

"I get up and nothin' gets me down
   You got it tough, I've seen the toughest around
   And I know, baby, just how you feel
   You got to roll with the punches and get to what's real"

Song 2

"The night is calling, I have to go
   The wolf is hungry, he runs the show
   He's licking his lips, he's ready to win
   On the hunt tonight for love at first sting"

Song 3

"She's a good girl, loves her mama
　　Loves Jesus and America, too
　　She's a good girl, who's crazy 'bout Elvis
　　Loves horses, and her boyfriend too"

Song 4

"I get up around seven
　　Get outta bed around nine
　　And I don't worry about nothin' no
　　'Cause worryin's a waste of my, time"

Song 5

"I've been burning, yes, I've been burning
　　Such a burden, this flame on my chest
　　No insurance to pay for the damage
　　Yeah, I've been burning up since you left"

Song 6

"She was a fast machine, she kept her motor clean
　　She was the best damn woman that I ever seen
　　She had the sightless eyes, telling me no lies
　　Knocking me out with those American thighs"

ROUND 4 – LYRIC TEST

Song 7

"If you rough it up
   If you like it you can slide it up
   Slide it up, slide it up, slide it up
   Don't make a grown man cry"

Song 8

"Cruised into a bar on the shore
   Her picture graced the grime on the door
   She's a long-lost love at first bite
   Baby, maybe you're wrong
   But you know it's all right, that's right"

Song 9

"They try to tell us we don't belong
   That's all right, we're millions strong
   This is my music, it makes me proud
   These are my people and this is my crowd"

Song 10

"I have climbed highest mountains
   I have run through the fields
   Only to be with you
   Only to be with you"

Round 4 Answers

1. Jump - Van Halen
2. Rock You Like a Hurricane - Scorpions
3. Free Fallin' - Tom Petty
4. Mr Brownstone - Guns N' Roses
5. Burning For You - Blue Oyster Cult
6. You Shook Me All Night Long - AC/DC
7. Start Me Up - The Rolling Stones
8. Dude (Looks Like a Lady) - Aerosmith
9. Crazy Crazy Nights - KISS
10. I Still Haven't Found What I'm Looking For - U2

Bonus Guitar Lesson 4

Scan the novelty sized QR code on the next page for your forth
Bonus Guitar lesson:
Back In Black - AC/DC. Main Guitar Riff

BONUS GUITAR LESSON 4

Chapter 5 - Indie/Alternative and Post-Punk Era

"Everybody was sort of going to sleep towards the end of 1983, and I felt that they had to be woken up!" - Morrissey

We are now heading into less mainstream genres of music. This will mean harder questions for many of you, depending on what music you're into. It also means fewer quiz rounds per chapter.

As we explored earlier, the 1980s was a decade of wealth, commercialism and elaborate fashion. Punk music never broke America in the 70s, and while many Punk Bands embraced the New Wave phenomenon, others stuck to their roots and kept their underground sound and cult status. Meanwhile, there were new Alternative bands forming that didn't embrace the Synth sound and elaborate fashion of the decade. Indie bands were largely still influenced by the music of the 1960s and 70s, and in the US, many got more radio play on college stations than in the mainstream. This music tends to be less 'of the time'.

Although Indie/ Alternative and Punk have very different sounds, what they do have in common is their underground movements. Independent bands and artists became hugely successful as the decade progressed, despite being signed to smaller record labels. These types of music

CHAPTER 5 - INDIE/ALTERNATIVE AND POST-PUNK ERA

gradually became more popular and by the end of the decade, gave birth to new genres like Grunge, as well as a more melodic and rhythm-guitar based Indie sound. These artists paved the way for the 1990s that would give birth to bands like Green Day, Blink 182, Oasis, Blur and many more.

The next few rounds are a mix of these genres, so let's find out how far beyond mainstream Pop your 80s music knowledge goes!

Ready?

Round 1

1. The Smiths had a hit with the 1984 single '_____ It Really Was Nothing'

- A. William
- B. Jonathan
- C. Nicholas
- D. Gregory

2. What was the name of the very first single by British Indie band The Stone Roses?

- A. Sally Cinnamon
- B. Elephant Stone
- C. Made Of Stone
- D. So Young

Fun Fact

Although their first official album came out in 1989, The Stone Roses actually formed in 1985 and began playing illegally in abandoned warehouses, gaining an underground following. They also released their first single in the same year on Thin Line. The band was so frustrated with their lack of notoriety that they began spray painting their band name all over Manchester. This earned them a bad reputation but, at the same time, gained them more attention from the music industry.

3. Which English Indie band had a hit single in 1988 with the song 'Crash'?

Fun Fact

The song was remixed in 1994 (The '95 mix) and used in the soundtrack for the film 'Dumb And Dumber' starring Jim Carey and Jeff Daniels.

4. What is the nickname of the dancer and mascot for The Happy Mondays?

Fun Fact

The Happy Mondays released their very long titled debut album 'Squirrel And G-Man Twenty Four Hour Party People Plastic Face Carnt Smile (While Out)' in 1987 but they formed in Manchester in 1980. They were pioneers in the merging of Indie Rock with Funk and House and made a name for themselves on the UK rave scene during the early to mid 80s.

5. What was the name of My Bloody Valentine's debut album?

6. Complete the band name 'Echo And The _____'

7. Which American band released the song 'Where Is My Mind?' in 1988?

Fun Fact

The band's frontman, Black Francis was inspired to write the song whilst scuba diving in the Caribbean. He recalls being chased by a very small fish at the time.

8. Can you name the first album R.E.M released after signing with Warner Bros in 1988?

Fun Fact

R.E.M became one of the world's biggest bands in the early 1990s. However, during the 1980s they were very much an underground college band that pioneered a return to a more traditional guitar-based music. They released 5 albums from 1983- 1987 without much mainstream success. It's only after signing with Warner Bros in 1988 that they began to gain this recognition. By 1991 they had finally claimed their first number 1 album in both the US and UK with 'Out Of Time' and became a household name.

ROUND 1

9. 'Teen Age Riot' was a hit single in 1988 by which American Rock band?

- A. Sonic Youth
- B. 9 Inch Nails
- C. The Smashing Pumpkins
- D. Nirvana

10. What was the debut single by the Scottish Indie band Jesus And Mary Chain?

- A. Darklands
- B. Upside Down
- C. Happy When It Rains
- D. Just Like Honey

Fun Fact

Bands like Jesus And Mary Chain, My Bloody Valentine, The Membranes and Primal Scream were all signed by Independent label Creation Records, founded in 1983 by Alan McGee. The label had some notoriety in the 80s but didn't achieve major success until they signed Oasis in 1993 who's second album '(What's The Story) Morning Glory' became the highest-selling UK album of the decade.

Round 1 Answers

1. William
2. So Young
3. The Primitives
4. Bez
5. Isn't Anything
6. Bunnymen
7. Pixies
8. Green
9. Sonic Youth
10. Upside Down

Round 2

1. Which of the following XTC songs is off their 1986 album 'Skylarking'?

- A. Making Plans For Nigel
- B. Ballad Of Peter Pumpkinhead
- C. Dear God
- D. Sense Of Working Overtime

2. Billy Corgan is the frontman for which Alternative Rock band formed in 1988?

Fun Fact

Before forming this band that would have major success in the 1990s, Corgan was in a Goth Rock band called 'The Marked'. After finding no success, he moved back to Chicago and played guitar in the band 'Deep Blue Dream' with future 'Static-X' frontman Wayne Static.

3. Which Alternative British Rock band was offered a record deal by Island records in the late 1980s, but decided they wanted to go to Oxford University to study first?

Fun fact

The band actually formed at school in 1985, but due to their choice to earn degrees before pursuing music careers, they didn't release their first EP 'Drill' until 1992. Their debut album 'Pablo Honey' was finally released in 1993.

4. What was the name of the Nine Inch Nails debut album in 1989?

5. Complete the 1982 hit single by The Jam off the album 'The Gift'

Town Called _____?

6. What is the name of the famous Christmas single released by The Pogues featuring Kirsty MaColl in 1988?

Fun Fact

Kirsty MaColl originally only went into the studio to record test vocals to see what the song would sound like as a duet. However, after hearing her performance, the band was so impressed they ended up keeping her vocals. Before Kirsty got the gig, lead singer Shane Macgowan suggested The Pretenders frontwoman Chrissie Hynde for the duet.

ROUND 2

7. Complete the following lyrics to the song that Kirsty MaColl covered in 1985.

"I don't want to change the world, I'm not looking for __ _____ _____"

Fun Fact

This song was originally written and released by singer/songwriter Billy Bragg in 1983 and also later covered by Green Day frontman Billie Joe Armstrong in 2020.

8. Name the frontman of the British Indie band, The Stone Roses.

9. Complete the song title released by Pixies in 1989.

'_____ Gone To Heaven'

10. What was the name of The Cure's lead singer, who was famous for his flamboyant long black hair and red lipstick?

Fun Fact

The Cure's lead singer first revealed this unique look during a dark period in the band's history while they were touring their 1982 album 'Pornography'. By the end of the tour, bassist Simon Gallup quit the band. During this period

Robert Smith described himself as a "monstrous person".

Round 2 Answers

1. Dear God
2. The Smashing Pumpkins
3. Radiohead
4. Nine Inch Nails
5. Town Called Malice
6. A Fairytale Of New York
7. A New England
8. Ian Brown
9. Monkey
10. Robert Smith

Round 3

1. Who sang the top 10 UK hit 'Real Wild Child (Wild One) in 1987?

Fun Fact

This song was originally recorded and released by Australian artist Johnny O'Keefe with The Deejays in 1958 and it was simply called 'Wild One'.

2. 'Should I Stay Or Should I Go' Was a hit single by which Punk band?

3. The Ramones 1980 album 'End of the Century' reached which number on the US Billboard chart?

- A. 11
- B. 32
- C. 44
- D. 67

ROUND 3

Fun Fact

Although a hugely influential Punk band, only 4 of the Ramones albums made it into the top 100 on the US Billboard.

4. Which band released the top 10 hit single 'Burning down the house' in 1983?

5. How many albums did the Dead Kennedys release during the 1980s?

- A. 3
- B. 4
- C. 5
- D. 6

Fun Fact

The Dead Kennedys were the first band to ever be brought to trial over some of the content of their 1985 album 'Frankenchrist'. It was by the Swiss artist H.R Giger known as 'The Penis Landscape' and depicted 3 close-up rows of men and women having sexual intercourse as an insert on the album cover. The image held nothing back and was seen as harmful to minors. The case resulted in a mistrial but was financially detrimental to the band and it was banned from multiple music stores in the United States. They broke up not long after.

6. The Misfits are known as the pioneers of the subgenre 'Horror Punk'. What image was on the front cover of their compilation album 'Collection' in 1986?

- A. Skull
- B. Devil
- C. Wolf
- D. Clown

Fun Fact

The Misfits took their name from the 1961 film 'The Misfits' starring Marilyn Monroe.

7. Which iconic 1971 film influenced the 1980s Punk band The Adicts bowler-hat wearing fashion sense?

8. The Punk Band Social Distortion formed in 1978 and was inspired by Punk legends 'The Sex Pistols'. In 1985 they took a brief break when lead vocalist Mike Ness went into a drug rehabilitation program. They Reformed in 1986 but didn't release their second album until 1988. What was the name of this album?

- A. Social Distortion
- B. Mommy's Little Monster
- C. Somewhere Between Heaven and Hell
- D. Prison Bound

ROUND 3

Fun Fact.

Social distortion has been talking about the release of an eight studio album since 2011, however, as of the release date of this book, this album has still yet to materialize.

9. Punk Band Bad Religion were formed in which American city in 1980?

- A. Los Angeles
- B. San Francisco
- C. Chicago
- D. New York

10. Who was the frontman of the Hardcore Punk band Minor Threat?

- A. Ian MacKaye
- B. Jeff Nelson
- C. Brian Baker
- D. Lyle Preslar

Round 3 Answers

1. Iggy Pop
2. The Clash
3. 44
4. Talking Heads
5. 4
6. Skull
7. A Clockwork Orange
8. Prison Bound
9. Los Angeles
10. Ian MacKaye

Round 4 – Lyric Test

Guess the song and artist by reading their words of wisdom.

Song 1

"Take me out tonight
   Where there's music and there's people
   And they're young and alive
   Driving in your car
   I never, never want to go home
   Because I haven't got one
   Anymore"

Song 2

"With your feet on the air and your head on the ground
   Try this trick and spin it, yeah
   Your head will collapse
   But there's nothing in it
   And you'll ask yourself"

Song 3

"You want it all, but you can't have it (Yeah, yeah, yeah)
  It's in your face, but you can't grab it (Yeah, yeah, yeah)"

Song 4

"I tried to laugh about it
  Cover it all up with lies
  I tried to laugh about it
  Hiding the tears in my eyes"

Song 5

"I'm not crazy - institution
  You're the one who's crazy - institution
  You're driving me crazy - institution
  They stuck me in an institution
  Said it was the only solution
  To give me the needed professional help
  To protect me from the enemy – myself"

Song 6

"Some people might say my life is in a rut
  I'm quite happy with what I got
  People might say that I should strive for more, but
  I'm so happy I can't see the point

ROUND 4 – LYRIC TEST

Something's happening here today
A show of strength with your boy's brigade"

Song 7

"Now the King told the boogie man
   You have to let that raga drop
   The oil down the desert way
   Has been shakin' to the top"

Song 8

"I can't seem to face up to the facts
   I'm tense and nervous and I can't relax
   I can't sleep 'cause my bed's on fire
   Don't touch me, I'm a real live wire"

Song 9

"Have you her have you heard
   The Way she plays there are no words
   To describe the way I feel
   How could it ever come to pass
   She'll be the first she'll be the last
   To describe the way I feel"

Song 10

"That's great, it starts with an earthquake
 Birds and snakes, and airplanes
 And Lenny Bruce is not afraid"

Round 4 Answers

1. There Is A Light And It Never Goes Out - The Smiths
2. Where Is My Mind - The Pixies
3. Epic - Faith No More
4. Boys Don't Cry - The Cure
5. Institutionalized - Suicidal Tendencies
6. Going Underground - The Jam
7. Rock The Casbah - The Clash
8. Psycho Killer - Talking Heads
9. She Bangs The Drums - The Stone Roses
10. It's The End Of The World As We Know It – R.E.M

Bonus Guitar Lesson 5

Scan the novelty sized QR code on the next page for your fifth
Bonus Guitar lesson:
This Charming Man - The Smiths. Intro Riff

BONUS GUITAR LESSON 5

Chapter 6 - Film and Television

"Any working composer or painter or sculptor will tell you that inspiration comes at the eighth hour of labour rather than as a bolt out of the blue. We have to get our vanities and our preconceptions out of the way and do the work in the time allotted" - John Williams

The 1980s was arguably the most creative and innovative decade for the film industry. Television was still evolving into what we know today, with a huge variety of incredible shows that focused on long-term storytelling. Although not aired until April 1990, the television show Twin Peaks - created and filmed at the end of the 1980s - was one of the first of its kind, blurring the line between film and television.

Thanks to film series like Star Wars, Rocky, Indiana Jones and The Terminator, movies became incredibly fun and entertaining. This led to an influx of action, fantasy and horror films. The 1980s was also the decade that the film soundtrack became incredibly popular, with pop bands and classical composers providing songs and scores that have become iconic.

In this chapter, you'll test your Film and TV knowledge and learn some more fun facts about the connection between music and the silver screen. Ready?

Round 1

1. What was the name of the theme song from the 1986 box office hit Top Gun?

Fun Fact

The song was written by Giorgio Moroder and Tom Witlock, who also wrote 'Take My Breath Away' which was also featured in the song.

2. The Breakfast club became a hugely successful movie in 1985. What was the name of the song and band featured in both the opening and closing credits?

3. Back To The Future featured the hit single 'Power Of Love'. Who was this song written and released by?

Fun fact

This artist also had a cameo in the scene where Marty Mcfly is auditioning for the high school battle of the bands.

4. Dolly Parton had a hit single in 1980. She also starred in the movie with the same title. What was the song called?

Fun Fact

Dolly still currently holds 2 Guinness World Records for 'Most Decades With a Top 20 Hit on the US Hot Country Songs Chart' and the 'Most Hits on U.S. Hot Country Songs Chart By a Female Artist'.

5. Which 1984 song did Prince sing that shares a name with a film released in the same year? It's also the film where Prince made his acting debut.

Fun Fact

Although most of us only think of Prince in reference to this song, he actually had a backing band - they were named 'Prince and the Revolution' between 1984-1987.

6. In 1985 Cindy Lauper released a song called ' _____ Are Good Enough'. This is also the title of the film it was written for. Name this song.

ROUND 1

7. Which Madness song was featured in the UK comedy show The Young Ones in the episode titled 'Sick' in 1984?

- A. It Must Be Love
- B. House Of Fun
- C. Our House
- D. Baggy Trousers

8. Both Rocky 3 in 1982 and Rocky 4 in 1985 boasted powerful soundtrack anthems from the Chicago-based Rock band 'Survivor'. Can you name both these songs?

9. '(I've Had) The Time Of My Life' was the main soundtrack for the 1987 film Dirty Dancing but which male and female duo sang this hit theme song?

10. The song 'Take My Breath Away' and the 1986 film Top Gun have become synonymous as the years have gone by. Which New Wave band named after a German city performed the song?

Fun Fact

'Take My Breath Away' was actually written by songwriters Giorgio Moroder and Tom Whitlock, who were not a part of the band.

Round 1 Answers

1. Danger Zone
2. Don't You (Forget About Me) - Simple Minds
3. Huey Lewis And The News
4. 9-5
5. Purple Rain
6. Goonies
7. Our House
8. Eye Of The Tiger and Burning Heart
9. Bill Medley and Jennifer Warnes
10. Berlin

Round 2

1. In Tim Burton's 1989 version of Batman, there is a classic scene where the Joker, played by Jack Nicholson defaces a variety of paintings and sculptures in the Gotham museum. Can you name the song and the artist who sings it?

2. Which British Rock band wrote and performed the entire soundtrack for the 1980 space opera movie Flash Gordon?

Fun Fact

Only one single from the album was released worldwide. It was simply called 'Flash'. It peaked at number 10 in the UK, 42 in the US, 3 in Germany but it managed to reach the number 1 slot in Austria.

3. The Irene Cara song 'What A Feeling' was in the soundtrack to which 1983 motion picture?

- A. The Breakfast Club
- B. Flashdance

- C. Dirty Dancing
- D. Cocktail

4. The line "Kick off the Sunday shoes" is from which 1984 film soundtrack? Hint: The song and the film have the same title.

5. All For Love, Cult Of Personality and In Your Eyes are all songs from which 1989 film starring John Cusack and Ione Skye?

6. ET, Indiana Jones and The Witches Of Eastwick are all film scores written by which composer?

7. In the 1984 film The Terminator there is a scene in which the song 'Burning In The Third Degree' is played. Where is this scene set?

- A. A bar
- B. A car chase
- C. A nightclub
- D. A fight in an abandoned factory

Fun Fact

Composer Brad Fiedel wrote and performed the iconic theme music for the film. The memorable 'clangs' we all know and love were recorded by Fiedel banging frying pans together. He then layered synthesizer melodies using Oberheim and Prophet 10 analog synths.

8. The iconic theme song to the Simpsons was written by which famous film and television composer?

- A. Danny Elfman
- B. John Williams
- C. Hans Zimmer
- D. Howard Shore

9. 'Bad Boy', 'The Minute I Saw You' and ' Daddy's Girl' are all songs from the soundtrack to which 1987 film starring Steve Guttenburg?

10. Randy Newman has provided the scores and soundtracks to countless classic films over the years. Which 1988 comedy used Randy's song 'I Love LA' during a baseball montage scene?

Fun Fact

As of September 2022 Newman has been nominated for 22 Academy Awards but won only 2 of them. He also won 3 Emmys, 7 Grammys and the Governor's Award from the Recording Academy. He is in the Songwriters Hall Of Fame, Rock 'N' Roll Hall Of Fame and in 2010 earned his star on the Hollywood Walk Of Fame.

Round 2 Answers

1. Partyman by Prince
2. Queen
3. Flashdance
4. Footloose
5. Say Anything
6. John Williams
7. A nightclub
8. Danny Elfman
9. 3 Men And A Baby
10. The Naked Gun

Fun Fact

Madonna was considered for the part of Ariel in Footloose. She hadn't broken through as an actress yet and she didn't make her acting debut until the 1985 film 'Desperately Seeking Susan'.

ROUND 2 ANSWERS

Fun Fact

As of this writing, John Williams has had more Oscar nominations than any living person in history. He currently sits at 52 nominations and 5 wins for Jaws, Star Wars, ET, Fiddler On The Roof and Schindler's List. He is the only person to receive nominations in seven decades.

Round 3

1. The 80's Glam Metal Band Dokken wrote the title song to 'A Nightmare On Elm Street 3'. What was the name of the song?

2. Which artist starred alongside Mel Gibson in the 1985 film 'Mad Max Beyond Thunderdome'?

3. 'We'll Always Be Together' is the line from the title soundtrack to which 1984 film? If you can name the song, then you can name the film.

4. Name the pop singer who sung the title song to the film 'The Neverending Story'

- A. Boy George
- B. Dan Seals
- C. Limahl
- D. Keith Sweat

ROUND 3

Fun Fact

Although incredibly cheesy, the song was a number 1 chart hit in Norway and Sweden. It also reached number 17 on the U.S. Billboard Hot 100, and sold more than 200,000 copies in the UK.

5. 'Put A Little Love In Your Heart' was from the soundtrack to which 1988 Christmas comedy starring Bill Murray?

Fun Fact

'Put A Little Love In Your Heart' was performed by Annie Lennox and Al Green for the film but was originally performed by Jackie Deshannon in 1969.

6. In 1985 Duran Duran wrote the title song to which James Bond film starring Roger Moore?

- A. For your eyes only
- B. Octopussy
- C. Moonraker
- D. A View To A Kill

7. What 1987 film was 'People Are Strange' by Echo And The Bunnymen used for?

8. Which member of Fleetwood Mac wrote the song 'Holiday Road' for the 1983 film National Lampoon's Vacation?

- A. Lindsey Buckingham
- B. Stevie Nicks
- C. Christine McVie
- D. Mick Fleetwood

9. The Jewel Of The Nile featured the soundtrack song 'When The Going Gets Tough, The Tough Get Going' in 1985. Who sang this classic?

10. What is the name of the band and main theme song to the 1987 film 'Mannequin'?

Round 3 Answers

1. Dream Warriors
2. Tina Turner
3. Electric Dreams
4. Limahl
5. Scrooged
6. A View To A Kill
7. The Lost Boys
8. Lindsey Buckingham
9. Billy Ocean
10. Nothing's Gonna Stop Us Now - Starship

Fun Fact

Tina Turner recorded two songs for the film 'We Don't Need Another Hero' and 'One Of The Living' which plays over the opening credits. We therefore hear Tina in the film before we see her.

Fun Fact

'Starship' was originally called 'Jefferson Airplane' then 'Jefferson Starship'. Nothing's Gonna Stop Us Now was their biggest hit, spending 1 week at number 1 in the US and 4 weeks in the UK.

Chapter 7 - Metal, Glam and Thrash

"If you leave me in a room long enough, I'll redecorate the room" - Nikki Sixx

Although its origins go back to the late 1960 and 1970s, it was in the 1980s that Heavy Metal really came into its own as a defined genre with subgenres including Glam Metal and Thrash. It's these three that we'll be testing our knowledge on in this chapter. Heavy Metal music is known for its fast, down-tuned guitar riffs, over-the-top hairstyles, and debaucherous behavior. It took Rock music to that next level of speed and aggression, particularly in Thrash Metal. During the 80s, Heavy Metal fans were often referred to as 'Headbangers' and 'Metalheads'.

Heavy Metal is more niche than mainstream Pop, so this could be a real test of your 80s knowledge. Let's delve deeper into Rock's most popular sub-genre of the decade.

Ready?

Round 1

1. Which Glam Metal band became famous for their spectacular live shows that featured pyrotechnics, roller coaster drums and flame thrower guitars?

2. In 1979 Ozzy Osbourne departed from Heavy Metal pioneers Black Sabbath. The band carried on and in 1980 released the critically acclaimed album 'Heaven And Hell'. Name the singer who replaced Osbourne?

Fun Fact

Sharon Arden, who was the daughter of Black Sabbath's manager Don Arden, recommended this singer to replace Ozzy. She would later marry the former frontman on July 4th 1982 to become Sharon Osbourne.

3. Which Motorhead album was released in 1980, reached number 4 in the UK charts and then achieved gold status in March of 1981?

ROUND 1

4. What was Judas Priest's highest-selling album?

   - A. Point Of Entry
   - B. Screaming For Vengeance
   - C. Defenders Of The Faith
   - D. Turbo

5. What year was Metallica's debut album 'Kill 'Em All' released?

   - A. 1981
   - B. 1982
   - C. 1983
   - D. 1984

6. What is the name of the famous, or should I say infamous, long-haired zombie-like skeleton on Iron Maiden's album covers?

   - A. Eddie The Head
   - B. Joey The Zombie
   - C. Eddie The Skull
   - D. Joey The Head

Fun Fact

Bruce Dickenson is a qualified pilot and has a tour plane that he flies himself called 'Ed Force One'. He was also expelled from boarding school for urinating in his head teacher's meal.

7. Which Swedish Glam Rock band released the multi-platinum album 'The Final Countdown' in 1986?

8. Name the Thrash Metal band that is named after an infectious disease that can and has been weaponized for biological warfare?

9. Which of these 'Slayer' albums was NOT released in the 1980s?

- A. Show No Mercy
- B. Seasons Of The Abyss
- C. Hell Awaits
- D. Reign In Blood

10. Which album was the Alice Cooper hit 'Poison' on?

- A. Trash
- B. Raise Your Fist And Yell
- C. DaDa
- D. Special Forces

Fun Fact

The early 1980s weren't as kind to Alice Cooper as the 1970s. His albums of this decade have been referred to as his "Blackout albums" as he apparently cannot remember recording them. He did, however, have better fortune as the decade progressed. The single 'Poison' was released in July 1989 and reached number 1 on the US Billboard chart and even higher in the UK at number 2.

Round 1 Answers

1. Motley Crew
2. Ronnie James Dio
3. Ace Of Spades
4. Screaming For Vengeance, *which has sold over 2,106,800 copies as of September 2022.*
5. 1983
6. Eddie The Head
7. Europe
8. Anthrax
9. Seasons Of The Abyss
10. Trash

Fun Fact

There are so many ridiculous facts about Motley Crew, it's hard to know where to start but here are just a few:

- *Nikki Sixx was declared legally dead for two minutes before resuscitation*

in 1987
- They threw furniture out of hotel rooms just for fun
- Tommy Lee and Vince Neil set fire to a hotel room with flare guns
- They were so out of control in the 80s that Gene Simmons from Kiss fired them from being their support act
- Tommy Lee and Pam Anderson married after knowing each other for just four days

Fun Fact

Motorhead's 'Killed By Death' Music video was banned in 1984 by MTV and it was considered too violent. The video shows Lemmy crashing his motorbike through a wall and flipping off his girlfriend's parents. He then gets chased and shot by the police and is then put onto the electric chair and executed. Finally, he rises from the grave by driving out of it on his bike.

Round 2

1. Who are the only two original band members of Metallica left?

- A. Lars Ulrich
- B. Dave Mustaine
- C. James Hetfield
- D. Ron McGovney

Fun Fact

Metallica has had 8 official members since forming in 1981.

2. The band Winger had two platinum albums during their career. One was the 1990 album 'In The Heart Of The Young'. Can you name the other released in 1988?

3. The 1989 debut album 'Dirty Rotten Filthy Stinking Rich' was by which Glam Metal Band?

4. Which Glam Metal band had the hit singles:

- Alone Again
- In My Dreams
- Burning Like A Flame

Fun Fact

During the filming of this band's music video 'Just Got Lucky' in Hawaii, guitarist George Lynch actually performed his shots on top of a smoking volcano. He only stopped once the lava started boiling and made it out unharmed. The volcano erupted 25 minutes later.

5. Which two of these four albums by the Death Metal band Carcass were released in the 1980s?

- A. Necroticism
- B. Symphonies Of Sickness
- C. Reek Of Putrefaction
- D. Heartwork

6. What year did Thrash Metal band Megadeth release their debut album 'Killing Is My Business…..And business Is Good'?

- A. 1983
- B. 1984
- C. 1985
- D. 1986

ROUND 2

Fun Fact

Megadeth's Dave Mustaine formed the band after being given to boot by his former band Metallica. His aim was to create a sound that was faster and more aggressive than Metallica. They soon became one of Heavy Metal's Big four along with Metallica, Slayer and Anthrax.

7. What was the name of Dio's first solo album?

Fun Fact

Dio began his music career as a Trumpet player and he played on stage with Gene Pitney when he was 15. He then became a singer, guitarist and bass player. He joined Black Sabbath from 1979 - 1982 before he released his first solo album in 1983. The title track from his first album was later parodied in the South Park episode 'Hooked on Monkey Fonics'. He describes this parody as "Wonderful"

8. 'Cum On Feel The Noize' was originally written and released by the British Rock band 'Slade' in 1973. 10 years later, it was covered by which American Heavy Metal band in 1983?

9. Which of the following Def Leppard songs was the only single to reach number 1 on the US Billboard chart?

- A. Hysteria
- B. Love Bites
- C. Animal
- D. Armageddon It

10. 'Here I Go Again' and 'Is This Love' are both hit singles by which Glam Metal band?

Round 2 Answers

1. Lars Ulrich and James Hetfield
2. Winger
3. Warrant
4. Dokken
5. Symphonies Of Sickness and Reek Of Putrefaction
6. 1985
7. Holy Diver
8. Quiet Riot
9. Love Bite
10. Whitesnake

Fun Fact

Quiet Riot was formed in 1973, the same year of the original Slade release. They broke up in 1980, reformed in 1982 and soon released their debut album the next year.

Round 3 – Lyric Test

Guess the song and artist by reading their words of wisdom.

Song 1

"Since I was born they couldn't hold me down
 Another misfit kid, another burned-out town
 I never played by the rules, I never really cared
 My nasty reputation takes me everywhere"

Song 2

"Pillage the village, trash the scene
 But better not take it out on me
 'Cause a ghost town is found
 Where your city used to be"

Song 3

"We've got the right to choose, and
 There ain't no way we'll lose it

This is our life, this is our song
We'll fight the powers that be, just
Don't pick on our destiny, 'cause
You don't know us, you don't belong"

Song 4

"Friday night and I need a fight
　My motorcycle and a switchblade knife
　Handful of grease in my hair feels right
　But what I need to make me tight are those"

Song 5

"The horse, he sweats with fear, we break to run
　The mighty roar of the Russian guns
　And as we race towards the human wall
　The screams of pain as my comrades fall"

Song 6

"Out on the streets, that's where we'll meet
　You make the night, I always cross the line
　Tighten our belts, abused ourselves
　Get in our way, we'll put you on your shelf"

Song 7

"Flash before my eyes
　Now it's time to die
　Burning in my brain
　I can feel the flame"

Song 8

"We both lie silently still
　In the dead of the night
　Although we both lie close together
　We feel miles apart inside"

Song 9

"When there's lightning, you know it always brings me down
　'Cause it's free and I see that it's me
　Who's lost and never found
　I cry out for magic, I feel it dancing in the light
　It was cold, I lost my hold
　To the shadows of the night"

Song 10

"What do you mean, "I couldn't be the President
　Of the United States of America"?
　Tell me something, it's still "We the people" right?"

Round 3 Answers

1. Youth Gone Wild - Skid Row
2. Cowboys From Hell - Pantera
3. We're Not Gonna Take It - Twisted Sister
4. Girls Girls Girls - Motley Crue
5. Iron Maiden - The Trooper
6. Round And Round - Ratt
7. Ride The Lightning - Metallica
8. Every Rose Has Its Thorn - Poison
9. Rainbow In The Dark - Dio
10. Peace Sells - Megadeth

Bonus Guitar Lesson 6

Scan the novelty sized QR code on the next page for your sixth Bonus Guitar lesson:
Sweet Child O' Mine - Guns N Roses. Main Riff

BONUS GUITAR LESSON 6

Chapter 8 - Music Video

"Music is forever; music should grow and mature with you, following you right on up until you die." — Paul Simon

Thanks to the advent of MTV and VH-1, music videos would become an essential tool for artists to get their music out to the people. Some artists were initially reluctant to use this new method to promote their sound, but others saw it as a chance to express themselves in a different way and on a bigger platform. Music videos became very elaborate and creative, emphasizing the unique fashion of the time. Actors from Hollywood and other forms of popular media were asked to star in many of these videos, giving them even more legitimacy in the eyes of the public. Some artists even used music videos as a means to create short films that went way beyond the typical three to four-minute Pop song.

In this short one-round chapter, I have described 10 music videos for you - so let's see how many of these classics you can remember!

Ready?

CHAPTER 8 - MUSIC VIDEO

1. Wrestling manager Captain Lou Albano appeared as her father in which 1983 Cindy Lauper music video?

Fun Fact

In the early-mid 1980s Cindy Lauper was famously a part of the Rock 'N' Wrestling Connection in which The World Wrestling Federation (now WWE) became heavily involved with MTV and Pop culture. Lauper was involved in multiple WWE appearances and was a part of the first Wrestlemania in 1985 along with celebrities like Muhammad Ali and Liberace.

2. Which 1985 Dire Straits video had a mix of the band performing on stage as well as multiple shots of various sporting blunders? One shot famously showed someone dancing dressed in a gorilla costume.

3. In this 1984 hit music video's main shots, the blonde female artist is wearing a pink dress, long pink gloves and boasting an incredibly large silver multi-diamond necklace. She is singing in a red room with red stairs with half a dozen men wearing black and white suits and two red stripes on their shirts. The video also begins with two men watching these shots in a cinema room smoking cigars.

4. Which 1984 music video starts with two rich businessmen in suits fighting in a sandpit surrounded by an audience frantically placing bets on the winner. By the end of the video, multiple fights have broken out. The video ends with the world blowing up.

5. Name the 1988 music video that shows a brunette female artist wearing a black dress and singing with a cartoon cat in the street, on a rooftop and on the stairs.

6. Which 1981 music video shows a female artist with short blonde hair in a gym comically working out with a mixture of very muscular and very fat men?

7. Name the provocative 1982 music video that shows a male artist with bleach blonde spikey hair slowly unveiling a long thin gray scarf in a gothic-looking church. The video also depicts someone's wedding day in this same church. By the end of the video, the bride is in a white dress, dancing in a kitchen with the singer. He is wearing red latex.

8. This next video starts with a young couple whose car has broken down. The boy turns into a werewolf when the moon rises. Later in the video, Zombies rise from their graves and proceed to dance with the male solo artist.

Fun Fact

The video cost half a million dollars to make, is almost 14 minutes long and was the most expensive music video ever to be made at the time. The working title was originally 'Starlight'.

9. Which 1985 'Tom Petty And The Heartbreakers' song depicts him as

the Mad Hatter in Alice In Wonderland and then Alice from becoming a sheet cake?

Fun Fact

Petty wrote the song with Eurythmics member Dave Stewart. It was inspired by and originally meant for Fleetwood Mac's Stevie Nicks after Stewart had a one-night stand with her in Los Angeles.

10. Name the song and artist from the 1982 song in which the band are partying in the Caribbean on a yacht, drinking, talking on pink and blue phones and lying in hammocks. It also shows a woman in multi-colored full body paint and a saxophone solo played on a raft.

Music Video Answers

1. Girls Just Wanna Have Fun - Cindy Lauper
2. Walk Of Life - Dire Straits
3. Material Girl - Madonna
4. Two Tribes - Frankie Goes To Hollywood
5. Opposites Attract - Paula Abdul
6. Physical - Olivia Newton-John
7. White Wedding - Billy Idol
8. Thriller - Michael Jackson
9. Don't Come Around Here No More - Tom Petty And The Heartbreakers
10. Rio - Duran Duran

Fun Fact

The name 'Frankie Goes To Hollywood' was stolen from an old American movie magazine headline that was reporting on Frank Sinatra moving to Tinsel Town.

Fun Fact

When auditioning for the LA Lakers at the age of 18, Paula Abdul stood out and caught the attention of the Jacksons. Due to this, she was hired as the choreographer on the music video for the song 'Torture'. She also worked on their 1984 Victory Tour.

Chapter 9 - Reggae/Ska

"One good thing about music, when it hits you, you feel no pain" - Bob Marley

Reggae music originated in the late 1960s in Jamaica and is linked to the Rastafari religion. Reggae has never been as popular in the West as Rock 'N' Roll or Hip Hop, but there have nevertheless been numerous breakthrough artists, with Bob Marley being the most well-known. Ska also originated in Jamaica in the late 1950s and was influenced by Rhythm and Blues, Jazz, Caribbean Mento, and Calypso. When Ska was brought to the UK, it evolved into sub-genres like 2-Tone, which blended Jamaican Ska with elements of Punk Rock. Many bands that blended elements of Reggae and Ska had huge hits during the 1980s.

In this chapter, you'll test yourself on traditional Reggae along with some popular Ska and 2-Tone bands from the decade. You'll also learn even more fun facts about these unique genres of music.

Ready?

Round 1

1. 'Don't Worry Be Happy' was a 1988 single released by which artist?

- A. Bob Marley
- B. Bobby McFerrin
- C. Bobby Womack
- D. Bobby Brown

2. Dave Wakeling was the singer and guitarist in which UK Ska band?

Fun fact

Wakeling was inspired to write the 1980 hit single 'Mirror In The Bathroom' when he was working in construction at the time and left his wet, sand-covered jeans on the bathroom floor overnight. It was winter and he wasn't keen to go to work wearing them so he started talking to himself in the mirror whilst shaving and feeling very isolated and self-involved. He made it to work in the end, but that moment led to him delving deeper into how self-involvement turns into narcissism. Then how narcissism turns into isolation and this cycle continues.

3. Which of these songs by The Specials spent 3 weeks at number 1 in the UK and 10 weeks in the top 40 in 1981?

- A. Ghost Town
- B. Rat Race
- C. Do Nothing
- D. I Can't Stand It

4. Complete the band name. Bob Marley And The _____?

5. 'Suggs' was the lead singer of which Ska band?

Fun fact

Suggs's real name is Graham McPherson and his band that formed in the late 1970s has had 15 top 10 singles in the UK alone.

Fun Fact

UB40 achieved huge success in their career, with over 70 million albums sold and over 50 singles in the UK charts. Their two most successful singles that reached number 1 in the UK and US were both cover versions. One was Elvis's 1961 hit 'Can't Help Falling In Love' released in 1993 and the other was a 1967 Neil Diamond song released in 1983.

6. Can you name this 1983 number 1 hit by UB40?

ROUND 1

7. Which UK Ska band released the following songs in the 1980s?

- Lip Up Fatty
- Special Brew
- Inner London Violence

8. Which Gregory Isaacs song released in 1980 was used in an advert for a cold and flu remedy to be taken before bedtime?

Fun Fact

As of September 2022, more than 500 Gregory Isaacs albums have been released.

9. Which Jamaican Reggae band toured with The Rolling Stones in the early 1980s and released the following Albums?

- Red
- Chill Out
- Anthem

Fun Fact

Rolling Stone magazine ranked 'Red' 23 in the top 100 albums of the 1980s. Anthem was released in 1984 and won the first-ever Grammy for best Reggae album the next year.

10. The Selecter's first run as a band from 1979 - 1982 was brief, however, they are considered one the most influential 2 Tone Ska bands of all time. What was the name of their second album in 1981?

Round 1 Answers

1. Bobby McFerrin
2. The Beat
3. Ghost Town
4. Wailers
5. Madness
6. Red Red Wine
7. Bad Manners
8. Night Nurse
9. Black Uhuru
10. Celebrate The Bullet

Round 2

1. In 1981 the Reggae band Scientist released their second album, that was named after a 1978 video game. Can you complete the album title?

'Scientists Meets The _____ _____

2. Which Reggae solo artist wrote and released the title soundtrack for the film 'Romancing The Stone in 1984?

3. 'Zungguzungguguzungguzeng' is the second studio album by which Reggae artist named after a color. Can you name him?

4. When Terry Hall, Neville Staple and Lynval Golding left 'The Specials' what was the name of the new band they formed?

5. What was the name of Bob Marley's final studio album in 1980?

ROUND 2

Fun fact

Bob Marley's birth name was 'Nesta Robert Marley'. He was actually a palm reader before he became a singer. He started at age four and stopped at age seven and never went back to it. He was also given a Peace Medal by the United Nations in 1978.

6. Which "Magical" 1981 single from their fourth album 'Ghost In The Machine' by 'The Police' reached number 1 in the Uk and number 3 in the US?

7. Which Reggae band released the hit single 'Strength Of My Life' in 1988?

8. Which 1985 song by Dennis Brown shares the same song name with The Beatles, The Cult, Robbie Williams, The Score and numerous other artists?

9. Sister Nancy Released a song in 1982 that shares the same name as a character from the cartoon The Flintstones. Can you name this song that is now regarded as a classic?

10. Which Bob Marley song only became known after the legend's death when the album 'Confrontation' was released in 1983?

Fun Fact

This song on his 13th studio album became one his best-known songs and is a classic to this day. The title is about the US Black Cavalry regiments that fought in the American Indian wars.

Round 2 Answers

1. Space Invaders
2. Eddy Grant
3. Yellowman, AKA King Yellowman
4. Fun Boy Three
5. Uprising
6. Every Little Thing She Does Is Magic
7. Israel Vibration
8. Revolution
9. Bam Bam
10. Buffalo Soldier

Fun Fact

Yellowman was born an Albino. Although he was shunned at first as his condition was not considered socially acceptable in Jamaica, he rose to fame and is considered one of Jamaica's great Reggae artists.

Fun Fact

Fun Boy Three had 6 top 20 chart hits, including top 10 hits like 'Our Lips Are Sealed' and 'Tunnel Of Love' and 'It Ain't What You Do, It's The Way You Do It'. They are also credited with helping launch the career of Bananarama as they provided the chorus vocals on this song. Fun Boy Three returned the favor and sang on the UK top 10 Bananarama song 'Really Saying Something'

Fun Fact

Every Little Thing She Does Is Magic was originally written in 1976 but the band didn't use it as it didn't have the Punk-Reggae-Rock sound that they were becoming known for. By the time the fourth album was ready, Sting felt that it could use a lighter song to compliment the heavier sound. The song then reached number 1 in the UK and number 3 in the US.

Round 3 – Lyric Test

Guess the song and artist by reading their words of wisdom.

Song 1

"Naughty boys in nasty schools
　Headmaster's breaking all the rules
　Having fun and playing fools
　Smashing up the woodwork tools"

Song 2

"Stop your messing around;
　Better think of your future,
　Time to straighten right out,
　Creating problems in town"

Song 3

"The night seems to fade

But the moonlight lingers on
There are wonders for everyone
The stars shine so bright
But they're fading after dawn
There is magic in ____ _____"

Song 4

"Old pirates, yes, they rob I,
   Sold I to the merchant ships,
   Minutes after they took I
   From the bottomless pit"

Song 5

"But I told her:
   Cool down the space for me little woman
   You're coming in to fast for me
   Cool down the space for me little woman
   That's not how it should be"

Song 6

"Guess there's no use in hangin' 'round
   Guess I'll get dressed and do the town
   I'll find a crowded avenue
   Though it will be empty without you"

ROUND 3 – LYRIC TEST

Song 7

"Young teacher, the subject
   Of schoolgirl fantasy
   She wants him so badly
   Knows what she wants to be"

Song 8

"I've got the stalk of _____
   Growing in my backyard
   I've got the stalk of _____
   Growing in my backyard"

Song 9

"Extraordinary, juice like a strawberry
   Money to burn baby, all of the time
   Cut to fit is me, fit to cut is she
   Come juggle with me, I say every time"

Song 10

"If you continue to burn up the
   Herbs, we gonna burn down the cane fields
   Soldier in the herb field, burnin the collie weed
   _____ __ _____, a search fi marijuana
   Policeman in the streets, searching fi collie weed"

Round 3 Answers

1. Baggy Trousers - Madness
2. A Message To You Rudy - The Specials
3. Kingston Town - UB40
4. Redemption Song - Bob Marley
5. Cool Down The Pace - Gregory Isaacs
6. Can't Used To Losing You - The Beat
7. Don't Stand So Close To Me - The Police
8. Sinsemilla - Black Uhuru
9. Here Comes The Hotstepper - Ini Kamoze
10. Police The Helicopter - John Holt

Bonus Guitar Lesson 7

Scan the novelty sized QR code on the next page for your seventh Bonus Guitar lesson: Redemption Song - Bob Marley

THE BIG 500 - 1980S MUSIC TRIVIA AND FUN FACTS

Chapter 10 - Soul/R&B

"To create something from nothing is one of the greatest feelings, and I would; I don't know, I wish it upon everybody. It's heaven" - Prince

Soul music originated in the late 1950s, and its musical roots came from Rhythm and Blues as well as African Gospel music. It became more popular during the civil rights movement in the 1960s and rapidly started to gain international popularity, heavily influencing a lot of popular music in the coming decades. The Motown record label formed in 1958 and signed some of the most successful artists in American history, becoming so big that it made Motown a sub-genre of Soul music in its own right.

R&B's roots developed from Rhythm and Blues music, but the lines between the two started to blur in the 80s, and R&B has since evolved into a genre in its own right. The two genres have incredibly different sounds - R&B is now often referred to as 'Rhythm and Bass', and is more focused on computer production than traditional musicianship. Much of the R&B music in the 1980s has a nice mix of both these elements and has produced some timeless classics.

Ready to test your Soul and R&B knowledge and learn some more fun facts?

Round 1

1. Which city in Mexico was the song title for the 1988 hit by Motown group The Four Tops?

2. Which of these Simply Red songs was NOT released in the 1980s?

    - A. Money's Too Tight To Mention
    - B. Holding Back The Years
    - C. Something Got Me Started
    - D. A New Flame

3. 'She Works Hard For The Money' spent three weeks at number 1 on the US Billboard R&B charts in 1983. Who sang this hit single?

4. Stevland Hardaway Judkins is the real name of which Soul singer?

5. Which of the following was the debut album of the R&B group New Edition?

ROUND 1

- A. All for Love
- B. Candy Girl
- C. Heart Break
- D. New Edition

6. Which Soul artist married the younger sister of Motown Founder Berry Gordy, making him an official member of the Motown Family? Hint- Their divorce inspired his final album ' Here My Dear'

Fun Fact

This artist was also a Motown Drummer, in a boy band, was in the US air force and even tried to join the NFL.

7. Which famous Motown girl group formed in Detroit that had the hits 'You Can't Hurry Love' and 'Stop! In The Name Of Love' was inducted into the Rock 'N' Roll Hall Of Fame in 1988?

8. The 1982 hit single 'A Night To Remember' was released by which group?

- A .Coffee
- B. The Whispers
- C. Lakeside
- D. Shalamar

9. Bill Withers had a hit single in 1981 that also won the Grammy for best R&B song in 1982. Was it...

- A. Ain't No Sunshine
- B. Just The Two Of Us
- C. Lovely Day
- D. Use Me

10. The 1988 debut single 'Fairplay' was released by which UK Soul group?

Round 1 Answers

1. Acapulco
2. Something Got Me Started
3. Donna Summer
4. Stevie Wonder
5. Candy Girl
6. Marvin Gaye
7. The Supremes
8. Shalamar
9. Just The Two Of Us
10. Soul ll Soul

Fun Fact

As a tribute to Dr Martin Luther King Jr, Stevie Wonder released the song 'Happy Birthday' in 1980, which also spearheaded the campaign to make Dr King's birthday a national holiday.

Fun fact

Motown legend Diana Ross's 1985 album 'Eaten Alive' was actually written by The Bee Gees and the single 'Chain Reaction' includes backing vocals by Barry Gibb himself.

Fun Fact

Shalamar member Jeffery Daniel was the first person to perform the now famous 'Moonwalk Dance' on the UK chart show 'Top Of The Pops' in 1982.

Round 2

1. 'I'm So Excited' was a smash hit single in 1984 by which Soul group?

Fun Fact

The song was originally released in 1982 but only peaked at number 30 on the US Billboard chart. It was remixed in 1984 and re-released to peak at number 9 in the US and number 11 in the UK.

2. Which R&B group was famously found out for lip-syncing at a "live performance" and later revealed that they were indeed imposters and never even sang on any of the songs?

Fun Fact

The group was first caught out on July 21st 1989 when performing the song 'Girl You Know It's True' at an MTV show in Bristol, Connecticut. The pre-recorded song started to skip and the "singers" began to panic. One of them even ran off the stage in humiliation. This was the beginning of the end for this group.

3. How many top 40 US Billboard singles did 'Kool And The Gang' have in 1985 from their 1984 album 'Emergency'?

- A. 2
- B. 3
- C. 4
- D. 5

Fun Fact

'Emergency" remains Kool And The Gang's highest-selling album to date with over 2 million copies sold in the US alone. They were the only band in 1985 to have all their singles from the album in the top 40.

4. Which artist released the single 'A House Is Not A Home' in 1981?

- A. Lionel Richie
- B. Stevie Wonder
- C. Barry White
- D. Luther Vandross

Fun Fact

By the age of just three years old, the singer in question had already started playing the piano. His parents luckily encourage his obvious musical talents.

ROUND 2

5. What was the name of Anita Baker's debut album in 1983?

- A. Rapture
- B. The Songstress
- C. Giving You The Best That I Got
- D. Rhythm Of Love

6. Which of the following songs was a hit-single duet with Aretha Franklin and George Michael?

- A. I Knew You Were Waiting For Me
- B. Jimmy Lee
- C. Willing To Forgive
- D. Get It Right

Fun Fact

Aretha Franklin's voice was so powerful and special that it was actually declared a "natural resource of the state" by the Department of Natural Resources of the state of Michigan in 1985. She was also the first woman to be inducted in the Rock 'N' Roll Hall Of Fame in 1987.

7. 'Smooth Operator' was a hit single by which Nigerian-born UK singer?

8. 'I Feel For You' was a breakthrough album for American singer Chaka Khan In 1984. The title track single was also a huge success but which

male artist originally wrote and released the song in 1979?

- A. Prince
- B. Morris Day
- C. Van Morrison
- D. Ben E. King

9. The 1986 James Brown album 'Gravity' featured which patriotic hit single?

Fun Fact

The Godfather of Soul performed the song in the 1985 movie Rocky 4. This exposure gave Brown his most successful single since his 1965 hit 'I Got You (I Feel Good)'. Rocky 4 was also the highest-grossing sports movie for over 24 years.

10. James Brown is known as The Godfather of Soul but who is known as The Godmother of Soul?

Fun fact

In 1984 The Godmother teamed with Soul legend Bobby Womack and released the hit single 'Love Has Finally Come At Last'

Round 2 Answers

1. The Pointer Sisters
2. Milli Vanilli
3. 4
4. Luther Vandross
5. The Songstress
6. I Knew You Were Waiting For Me
7. Sade
8. Prince
9. Living In America
10. Patti LaBelle

Round 3 – Lyric Test

Song 1

"Baby, I got sick this mornin' (heal me my darling, heal me my darling)
   A sea was stormin' inside of me
   Baby, I think I'm capsizin'(heal me my darling, heal me my darling)
   The waves are risin' and risin'"

Song 2

"Remember when you first found love how you felt so good?
   Kind that last forever more so you thought it would
   Suddenly the things you see got you hurt so bad, so bad
   How come the things that make us happy make us sad
   It seems to me that"

Song 3

"You better run, you better do what you can
   Don't wanna see no blood, don't be a macho man
   You wanna be tough, better do what you can

ROUND 3 – LYRIC TEST

So beat it, but you wanna be bad"

Song 4 - Duet

"My love, there's only you in my life
   The only thing that's right"

"My first love
   You're every breath that I take
   You're every step I make"

Song 5

"No April rain, no flowers bloom
   No wedding Saturday within the month of June
   But what it is, is something true
   Made up of these three words that I must say to you"

Song 6

"Gotta let you know girl you're looking good
   You're out of sight, you're alright
   Tell the DJ to play your favorite tune
   Then you know it's okay
   What you found is happiness, now"

Song 7

"I'm never gonna dance again
　　Guilty feet have got no rhythm
　　Though it's easy to pretend
　　I know you're not a fool"

Song 8

"Hey everybody in the neighborhood
　　The beauty's on duty, better hear me good
　　Sister e-flat tomato, brother b-flat balloon
　　Somethin' funky's goin' down, better listen to my tune"

Song 9

"She likes the boys in the band
　　She says that I'm her all-time favorite
　　When I make my move to her room, it's the right time
　　She's never hard to please"

Song 10

"Cause I wonder where you are and I wonder what you do
　　Are you somewhere feeling lonely or is someone loving you?
　　Tell me how to win your heart, for I haven't got a clue
　　But let me start by saying, I love you"

Round 3 Answers

1. Sexual Healing - Marvin Gaye
2. Joy And Pain - M.A.Z.E featuring Frankie Beverly
3. Beat it - Michael Jackson
4. Endless Love - Lionel Richie and Diana Ross
5. I just Called To Say I Love You - Stevie Wonder
6. Let's Groove - Earth, Wind and Fire
7. Careless Whisper - George Michael
8. The Dude - Quincy Jones
9. Super Freak - Rick James
10. Hello - Lionel Richie

Bonus Guitar Lesson 8

Scan the novelty sized QR code on the next page for your eighth Bonus Guitar lesson:
Beat It - Michael Jackson

BONUS GUITAR LESSON 8

Chapter 11 - Album Cover Description

"I try to explain that to my kids - the experience of going to a record store, flipping through racks and finding that album cover that intrigues you - but my kids don't want to know about it. They download the one song on the album they like, and pay their 99 cents" – Jon Bon Jovi

As the decade has evolved with music, so have the extra touches that make a great band or artist become legendary. It's no surprise then that the 1980s led to some of the most iconic and creative album titles and covers of all time. The band or artist didn't even need to be on the cover to make them eye-catching and memorable. In the 1960s and 1970s there were iconic album covers like Sgt. Pepper's Lonely Hearts Club Band and Pink Floyd's Dark Side Of The Moon but what about the 80s?

Well now it's time to find out how well you remember those classic albums that you lined up for hours in record stores to get your hands on.

Ready?

CHAPTER 11 - ALBUM COVER DESCRIPTION

1. Which Metallica album cover depicts a pair of hands in a cloudy blood-red sky manipulating rows of white crosses with string?

Fun Fact

Painter Don Brautigam designed the album cover based on a concept by the band and their manager Peter Mensch. Brautigam was also the artist who designed the cover for Stephen King's 'The Stand' in 1980.

2. Which 1989 British Indie bands album cover features Jackson Pollock-Esque paint splats in the background with 3 horizontal stripes of red, white and blue on the middle left-hand side and 3 slices of lemon?

3. Which Kate Bush album cover had her lying down on a purple backdrop wearing a purple dress and hugging two Weimaraner dogs?

Fun Fact

The two dogs were Bush's friends' and called Bonnie and Clyde and her brother John was the photographer.

4. In 1985 The Smiths released an album with a black and white cover showing a young soldier wearing a hard army hat. The title of the album is written on the hat. Can you name it?

Fun Fact

The band was named 'The Smiths' because Morrisey wanted something as simple as possible at a time when band names were lavish, pretentious or just very long. When interviewed on kids TV show DataRun in 1984, Morrissey said: "I decided on The Smiths because it was the most ordinary name, and I thought it's time that the ordinary folk of the world showed their faces".

5. Which 1987 Prince album shows a mustard yellow drum kit, set up on a stage with a backdrop of a city street? On the floor is a pink guitar and Prince himself looks to be walking out of the shot and out of focus.

Fun Fact

The backdrop from this classic album cover was from a Minneapolis production of 'Guys and Dolls'

6. Name the 1984 album cover that shows a man with his back to the camera from his thighs to shoulders. He's wearing a white T-shirt, blue jeans, studded belt and he has a red cap hanging out of his right back pocket. The backdrop is the red and white stripes from the American flag.

7. Which 1980s New Wave band's album cover shows four individual portraits of the band members? All their faces are blotted out with red blocks and the letters 'A' of the band's name at the top of the cover are upside down.

CHAPTER 11 - ALBUM COVER DESCRIPTION

8. Which Van Halen album features a painting of a young boy with angel wings smoking a cigarette?

9. Name the 1987 Pink Floyd album that shows multiple rows of brown metal framed beds on a beach stretching as far as the eye can see. There is a man sitting on one of the beds in the center of the cover.

Fun Fact

This cover was made before the luxury of photoshop or CGI so 700 beds had to be laid out on the beach at the cost of over $500,000.

10. Which 1983 David Bowie album showed him on the cover standing in a boxing stance wearing thin black gloves with a silhouette of a city in the background and the shadow of himself?

Fun Fact

Bowie turned down a knighthood from The Queen twice and also a role as the villain in the 1985 James Bond film 'A View To A Kill'.

Album Covers Answers

1. Master Of Puppets - Metallica
2. The Stone Roses - The Stone Roses
3. Hounds Of Love - Kate Bush
4. Meat Is Murder - The Smiths
5. Sign O' The Times - Prince
6. Born In The USA - Bruce Springsteen
7. Remain In Light - Talking Heads
8. 1984 - Van Halen
9. A Momentary Lapse Of Reason - Pink Floyd
10. Let's Dance - David Bowie

Bonus Guitar Lesson 9

Scan the novelty sized QR code on the next page for your ninth Bonus Guitar lesson: That's Entertainment - The Jam

THE BIG 500 - 1980S MUSIC TRIVIA AND FUN FACTS

Chapter 12 – Hip-Hop And Early Gangsta Rap

"Hip-hop has always been chronologically misunderstood. Too many times, people are hearing the story from the second floor. Nobody's heard the story from the basement. If hip-hop was a cake, all I can tell you is the eggs, the flour, the sugar, the vanilla - the ingredient years" - Grandmaster Flash.

Hip-Hop music originated in the Bronx, NYC, in the 1970s. Unlike Rock, its music is based on rhythmic drum loops, referred to as 'Beats' and the vocals mostly use rapping instead of singing to express themselves. The 'catch' of the songs are often sampled from previous chart hits to add commercialism, familiarity and nostalgia.

Hip-Hop was still a long way from becoming one of the most popular music genres in the world, but the 1980s was undoubtedly the decade of Rap's pioneers. These artists paved the way for future rappers like Eminem, Jay Z, Kanye West, Busta Rhymes and many more who would emerge post-1980s. You'll see that as the decade rolls on, the birth of 'Gangsta Rap' emerges from the streets of both the East and West coast of the United States. These artists would soon become some of the most successful rappers in history.

If you are a 1980s Hip-Hop fan, then this is what you've been waiting for!

Ready?

Round 1

1. Kurtis Blow was the first rapper to sign a record contract with a major label. What was the name of the first Hip-Hop single that went gold?

- A. The Ride
- B. The Breaks
- C. The Chain
- D. The Drive

2. What was the name of the first Hip-hop group to feature a female rapper?

- A. Salt -N- Pepa
- B. Run DMC
- C. Funky Four Plus One
- D. N. W. A

3. Grandmaster Flash and the Furious Five's hit single 'The message' is considered one of the most important Hip-Hop singles of all time. What year was it released?

- A. 1981
- B. 1982
- C. 1983
- D. 1984

Fun Fact

Grandmaster Flash was the first DJ to experiment with two turntables and after becoming a "Grandmaster" at that, he then began to scratch vinyl with his hands behind his back.

4. Which Hip-Hop artist collaborated with Rock Band Aerosmith in 1986 with the song 'Walk this way'?

Fun fact.

Walk this way was actually originally released in 1975 on the hit Aerosmith album 'Toys in the Attic' The single peaked on the billboard chart at number 10 in early 1977. The new version had even more chart success and peaked at number 4 in the US and number 8 in the UK.

5. What was the name of Whodini's second studio album?

- A. Back in Black
- B. Six
- C. Open Sesame
- D. Escape

ROUND 1

6. Which Hip-Hop label did LL Cool J sign with in 1984?

- A. Def Jam Records
- B. Bad Boy Records
- C. Sugar Hill Records
- D. Jive Records

7. The Beastie boys are known as a Rap/Rock group and formed in 1981. What was the name of their famous single in 1986 that was all about 'partying'?

Fun fact.

The 'Beastie' in Beastie Boys was originally an acronym that stood for 'Boys Entering Anarchistic States Towards Inner Excellence'. As you can imagine, this made no sense when having another 'Boys' at the end. It was also inaccurate as one of their founding members was a female drummer called Kate Schellenbach.

8. Which of these Gangsta rappers was not a part of the N.W.A?

- A. Dre Dre
- B. Snoop Dogg
- C. Easy E
- D. Big Daddy Kane

9. How many members were there of the Rap group Salt-N-Pepa?

- A. 2
- B. 3
- C. 4
- D. 6

Fun fact

On Salt-N-Pepa's 1986 debut album 'Hot, cool and vicious' 'Push it' did not find its way on there. It was originally a B-side on the single 'Tramp' in 1987 and then later as its own single in 1988, peaking at number 19 on the Billboard chart that same year. VH1 later ranked it number 9 on its hundred greatest songs of Hip-Hop.

10. In 1987 Public Enemy released perhaps their most influential album 'It Takes A Nation Of Millions To Hold Us Back'. The first single's title of this groundbreaking album was a 'pun' of an old saying "Devil Without a Cause".

What word replaced "Cause"?

Round 1 Answers

1. The Breaks
2. Funky Four Plus One
3. 1982
4. Run-D.M.C
5. Escape
6. Def Jam records
7. Fight For Your Right
8. Big Daddy Kane
9. 3
10. Pause

Fun Fact

Run-D.M.C is known as the 'Kings of Hip-Hop'. They have sold over 230 million records to date and were first group in Hip-Hop to reach numerous accomplishments including

- *First Hip-Hop group on the cover of Rolling Stone*
- *First to have a platinum album 'Raising Hell'*

- *First to have a Hip-Hop video on MTV*
- *First to achieve a Grammy nomination*
- *First Hip-Hop group to earn gold, platinum and multi-platinum albums*

Round 2

1. Complete the Rap duo who released their debut album 'Paid In Full' in 1987.

Eric B. & _____

2. EPMD's hit 1988 single 'You Gots To Chill' was off which album?

- A. Business As Usual
- B. Business Never Personal
- C. Strictly Business
- D. Unfinished Business

3. Finish the name of this classic N.W.A album. 'Straight Outta _____

- A. Philly
- B. Compton
- C. LA
- D. Oakland

Fun Fact

After opening for Salt 'N' Pepa during a 1987 tour, Ice Cube decided that he wanted to go back to college to get a diploma in architectural drafting and design. The Rap scene was still not booming like it soon would. He did return to The N.W.A in September 1988 after writing two new songs for Eazy-E's solo debut album.

4. Were Public Enemy an East coast or West coast Hip-Hop group?

Fun Fact

One of their breakthrough songs 'Fight The Power' was the theme song for the soundtrack to Spike Lee's 1989 film 'Do The Right Thing'.

5. Richard Martin Lloyd Walters is also known as which Hip-Hop artist?

Fun Fact

Walters was the third artist to be signed by Death Jam records and his music has been sampled over a thousand times by artists such as Eminem, The Beastie Boys, Kanye West, Beyonce and many more!

6. Jeff Townes and Will Smith were a DJ and Rap duo from mid 1985 - 1994. They had various hit singles in the 80s including 'Parents Don't Understand'. What was their stage name?

ROUND 2

7. 'All Hail The Queen' was a debut Rap album released in 1989 but who was the Queen?

8. Which single by The Sugarhill Gang reached number 36 on the US Billboard chart on January 12th 1980?

- A. Apache
- B. Rappers Delight
- C. Radio Commercial
- D. Sugar Hill Grove

Fun Fact

This song was the first Rap single to ever reach the top 40 on the US billboard.

9. In 1988 KRS- One was part of which Hip-Hop group that released the album 'By All Means Necessary'?

Fun Fact

KRS- One is an acronym for 'Knowledge Reigns Supreme Over Nearly Everyone'

10. Which Kool Moe Dee single was a hit in 1988 and later sampled by the Will Smith song in 1999 with the same name? Smith also starred in the film, which also shared the same name?

Round 2 Answers

1. Rakim
2. Strictly Business
3. Compton
4. East Coast
5. Slick Rick
6. DJ Jazzy Jeff And The Fresh Prince
7. Queen Latifah
8. Rappers Delight
9. Boogie Town Productions
10. Wild Wild West

Fun Fact

Eric B. & Rakim's first single 'Eric B Is President' was the first time a James Brown song was sampled, with the hit 'Funky President'.

Fun Fact

Queen Latifah's debut album in 1989 titled 'All Hail To The Queen' went on

ROUND 2 ANSWERS

to sell over a million copies.

Round 3 – Lyric Test

Song 1

"We rock and don't stop
　Well, it's the supercalifragilisticexpialidocious
　With no strings attached, no bags of tricks
　This is the way we get our kicks"

Song 2

"We're gonna prove to the world that we're the real
　We're gonna prove to everybody we know the real deal
　We got golden voices and hearts of steel
　'Cause we're five emcees that got to be real"

Song 3

"Two years ago, a friend of mine
　Asked me to say some MC rhymes
　So I said this rhyme I'm about to say
　The rhyme was Def a-then it went this way"

ROUND 3 – LYRIC TEST

Song 4

"It's like a jungle sometimes
  It makes me wonder how I keep from going under
  It's like a jungle sometimes
  It makes me wonder how I keep from going under"

Song 5

"You've been waitin' and debatin' for oh so long
  Just starvin' like Marvin for a Cool J Song
  If you cried and thought I died, you definitely was wrong
  It took a thought, plus I brought Cut Creator along"

Song 6

"Gold on my neck my pistols close at hand
  I'm a self-made monster of the city streets
  Remotely controlled by hard Hip-Hop beats
  But just livin' in the city is a serious task
  Didn't know what the cops wanted
  Didn't have the time to ask
  Word"

Song 7

"Now, now, now, wait a minute y'all
  This dance ain't for everybody

Only the sexy people
So all you fly mother's, get on out there and dance
Dance, I said"

Song 8

"Yet our best trained, best educated, best equipped
Best prepared troops refuse to fight
As a matter of fact, it's safe to say that they would rather switch
Than fight"

Song 9

"I'm your idol the highest title numero uno
I'm not a Puerto Rican but I'm speakin so that you know
And understand I got the gift of speech
And it's a blessin
So listen to the lesson I preach"

Song 10

"Ultra {magnetic, magnetic}
MC's Ultra {magnetic, magnetic}
MC's Ultra {magnetic, magnetic} MC's
Kool Keith!"

Round 3 Answers

1. New Rap Language - Treacherous Three
2. That's The Joint - Funky Four Plus One
3. Sucker MC's - Run – D.M.C
4. The Message - Grandmaster Flash And The Furious Five
5. Rock The Bells - LL Cool J
6. 6 'N The Mornin
7. Push It - Salt And Pepper
8. Fight The Power - Public Enemy
9. I got It Made - Special Ed
10. Ego Trippin - Ultramagnetic MC's

Chapter 13 - Big events, Awards and Chart Toppers

"I'm never pleased with anything, I'm a perfectionist, it's part of who I am" – Michael Jackson

In our final chapter, we're going to take a look at some more important dates in 1980s music history, as well as some chart toppers and artistic accomplishments. The 80s have produced some of the biggest bands and artists of all time and you're about to see just how monumental some of these events and musical accomplishments were.

Ready for your final questions and fun facts?

1. The highest-selling single of the 1980s in the UK was?

- A. Cindy Lauper - Girls Just Wanna Have Fun
- B. Madonna - Holiday
- C. Band aid - Do They Know It's Christmas
- D. The Jam - That's Entertainment

CHAPTER 13 - BIG EVENTS, AWARDS AND CHART TOPPERS

2. MTV was revolutionary and changed the music industry forever. What year was it launched?

- A. 1980
- B. 1981
- C. 1982
- D. 1983

3. What was the first music video to be aired on MTV in the United States?

- A. You Don't Want Me- Human League
- B. Kids In America - Kim Wilde
- C. In The Air Tonight - Phil Collins
- D. Video Killed The Radio Star - The Buggles

4. Who is the highest-selling Heavy Metal band in history that formed in the 1980s?

- A. Iron Maiden
- B. Black Sabbath
- C. Judas Priest
- D. Metallica

5. On July 13th 1985 both Wembley Stadium, London and John F. Kennedy Stadium, Philadelphia, hosted a huge multi-venue fundraiser concert. What was the name of this historic event?

6. Which legendary Rock band broke up on 25th September 1980 after drummer John Bonham died of alcohol poisoning at the age of 32? He apparently drank 40 shots of vodka in one day.

7. What was the highest-selling album of the 1980s that sold over 66 million copies?

Fun fact

The artist who released this album was also the highest-selling artist of the decade.

8. Which female artist caused major controversy by rising out of a giant wedding cake, flashing her underwear and garters at the MTV Video Music Awards on 14th September 1984?

9. In what city was John Lennon murdered on 8th December 1980?

10. What movie about a Spoof Rock band premiered on 2nd March 1984?

Big events, Awards and Chart Toppers Answers

1. Band Aid - Do they know it's Christmas with over 11,700,000 worldwide sales to date.
2. 1981
3. Video Killed The Radio Star - The Buggles
4. Metallica
5. Live Aid
6. Led Zeppelin
7. Thriller - Michael Jackson
8. Madonna
9. New York
10. Spinal Tap

Fun Fact

Most of 'Do they know it's Christmas' was recorded and mixed on Sunday, November 25 1984 in under 24 hours at Sarm West Studios in London. Simon LeBon and Sting recorded their vocals before the day but all the other artists came on the 25th.

Fun Fact

One of The Buggles founders was Trevor Horn who also joined the band 'Yes' and sang lead vocals and played fretless bass on the album 'Drama' in 1980. Horn then went on to become a full time producer working with 'Frankie Goes To Hollywood', 'Propaganda', and 'Art Of Noise' to name just a few.

Fun Fact

As of this publication, Metallica has sold over 100 million albums worldwide. They have played over 2000 gigs and counting. The US city they have played in the most is San Francisco and the country outside the US is Germany.

Fun Fact

Phil Collins was the only artist to perform at both Live Aid venues at Wembley in London and JFK in Philadelphia. He quickly crossed the Pond on a Concorde and made it in time to play for the American audience.

Fun Fact

Although Spinal Tap were hailed as 'One of England's loudest bands' three of the members, Michael Mckeen, Christopher Guest and Harry Shearer were all American. Shearer is best known as the voice of Mr Burns, Ned Flanders and others on the TV show The Simpsons.

10 Final Fun Facts About the 1980s

You can relax now and enjoy 10 final fun facts about this phenomenal decade.

1. In March 1980 the Tbilisi Rock Festival was held. This was the first state-sanctioned rock music festival in the Soviet Union.

2. The Heavy Metal magazine 'Kerrang' published its first-ever edition in June 1981. It featured Angus Young from AC/DC on the front cover.

3. In September 1981 Simon & Garfunkel reunited for a free gig in Central Park, NYC. Over 500,000 people reportedly came to this historic concert. Over the years this number has been disputed, so it's hard to know the exact attendance but the photos taken on the day clearly show the mass scale of this event.

4. In October 1982 the very first CD player was available for consumer consumption in Japan. It was the Sony CDP-101. CDs then became available in the USA the next year. By 1985 the Dire Straits album

'Brothers in Arms' became the first record to sell more CDs than Vinyl.

5. In 1984 MTV hosted the first annual MTV Music Video Awards in New York City. The Cars song 'You Might Think' won Video Of The Year, whilst Michael Jackson, Cindy Lauper, ZZ Top, Eurythmics, David Bowie, Herbie Hancock, The Police and Van Halen also won awards.

6. On January 1st 1985 the music channel VH-1 broadcast for the very first time in the USA. Marvin Gaye kicked off this broadcast with a video performance of The Star-Spangled Banner. VH-1 was aimed at the softer side of popular music at the time, as well as playing older hits using concert and newsreel footage.

7. In 1985 'We Are The World' by 'USA for Africa' was released. It was written by Michael Jackson and Lionel Ritchie and produced by Quincy Jones and was a Supergroup consisting of a huge array of talent. Billy Joel, Willie Nelson, Tina Turner, Bruce Springsteen, Huey Lewis, Bob Dylan, Stevie Wonder, Cyndi Lauper, Ray Charles, Diana Ross, Steve Perry, Lindsey Buckingham, Smokey Robinson, Kenny Rogers and Kim Carnes are among the names that performed on this record.

8. In September 1985 Michael Jackson outbid Sir Paul McCartney to buy the rights to The Beatles back-catalog for $47 million. It wasn't until 2008 that Jackson gave up the catalog to Sony.

9. On August 1st 1987 MTV Europe was officially launched. It kicked

10 FINAL FUN FACTS ABOUT THE 1980S

off with broadcasting an Elton John concert from Amsterdam and 'Money for Nothing' by Dire Straits was the first music video to air.

10. In 1988 The Beatles (inducted by Mick Jagger), The Drifters (inducted by Billy Joel), The Beach Boys (Inducted by Elton John), The Supremes (inducted by Little Richard) and Bob Dylan (inducted by Bruce Springsteen) all took their rightful places in the Rock 'N' Roll Hall Of Fame.

Bonus Guitar Lesson 10

Scan the novelty sized QR code on the next page for your tenth Bonus Guitar lesson:
Summer Of 69 - Bryan Adams

BONUS GUITAR LESSON 10

Chapter 14 - What Comes Next?

As we've seen in the last 13 chapters, the 1980s was truly a unique decade of music opening up the creative envelope and expanding into new musical genres that are still thriving today.

Thanks to the 1980s, Rock music continued to grow and evolve, and graced us with some of the greatest bands of all time throughout the 90s and beyond. Hip Hop would soon become almost as popular as Rock 'N' Roll, and the two even started to mix styles creating genres like Rap Rock and Nu Metal as the new millennium came closer. Punk music finally became more mainstream in the United States, and the Pop Punk genre developed with bands like Blink-182, Sum-41 and My Chemical Romance becoming extremely popular.

Mainstream Synth Pop mostly laid dormant during the 90s and early 2000s, but artists like Daft Punk, Sebastien Tellier and Chromeo didn't let us forget about this unique 80s sound. In many ways, it came full circle in the mid 2000s when bands like The Killers and Two Door Cinema Club brought back the use of synthesizers into the mainstream charts once again.

Pop music would progressively become far more manufactured as the years rolled on, and the 90s would be the final decade before the digital

CHAPTER 14 - WHAT COMES NEXT?

era, which made any music available at the touch of a button. We can now enjoy music from the 80s whenever we get the urge for nostalgia, whether it be at home, at a party or in the gym.

The 80s was, without a doubt, a decade of passion, vibrance and expression in ways that had never been seen before. It was a time of musical freedom and originality. Fashion, MTV and the advent of music videos played a huge role in giving the artists of the 1980s international exposure and a chance for their fans to experience these now classic hits visually and well as musically. What a groundbreaking time in Pop culture history it was!

I hope you've enjoyed testing your knowledge and learning some new fun facts about one of the greatest Pop culture decades. Reviews are a huge help for me so be sure to leave me one on Amazon and check out my other Big 500 music books on past and future decades when they are published.

Being such an incredibly diverse decade of music, I'm well aware that there is so much else to explore and many more questions to be tested on. So, on topic of future 1980s trivia books to come, all I can say is . . .

I'll be back.

Where To Find Me

To keep updated on future books, find more information about online guitar lessons, and to check out my own original music, go to www.nickswettenhammusic.com or scan the novelty sized QR code on the next page.

WHERE TO FIND ME

www.ingramcontent.com/pod-product-compliance
Lightning Source LLC
Chambersburg PA
CBHW030035100526
44590CB00011B/220